"Don Delves is one of the industry's most knowledgeable compensation consultants. His book makes an important contribution to the stock option dialogue."—**Larry Hirsch, Chairman & CEO of Centex Corporation**

"This is an excellent book for anyone interested in the important discussion of stock option expensing and, more significantly, the optimal use of stock options in compensation plans. It is written from the point of view of an experienced and knowledgeable compensation consultant who has advised board compensation committees and talked with many people outside the field considering the economic and incentive effects of the overuse of stock options in the 90s."—**John M. Biggs, former Chairman & CEO of TIAA-CREF**

"This book is very thoughtful and insightful. There are no right answers– only degrees of balance. The author has achieved that well."—**John Rau, President and CEO of Miami Corporation; former CEO of Chicago Title & Trust Company**

"If you are on the Compensation or Finance Committee of a Board, this is a must read. With the portfolio of executive compensation Don Delves assisted us with, BorgWarner has risen to the top without megagrants of stock options."—**John F. Fiedler, former Chairman and CEO of BorgWarner**

"Don Delves has given us a clear, lively exposition of multiple issues and variables to be considered in formulating incentives to improve corporate and executive performance. Along with his unequivocal advocacy of expensing stock options, he calls for a more balanced approach to compensation, one that blends a variety of elements to engender more attention on the long-term health of the enterprise. His interviews with thought leaders such as Paul Volcker and Myron Scholes and the incisive questions he poses help frame a robust debate on the proper use of options."—**Ronald L. Turner, Chairman, President, and CEO of Ceridian Corporation**

STOCK OPTIONS AND THE NEW RULES OF CORPORATE ACCOUNTABILITY

Measuring, Managing, and Rewarding Executive Performance

DONALD P. DELVES

McGraw-Hill

New York   Chicago   San Francisco   Lisbon
London   Madrid   Mexico City   Milan
New Delhi   San Juan   Seoul
Singapore   Sydney   Toronto

The McGraw·Hill Companies

Library of Congress Cataloging-in-Publication Data
Delves, Donald P.
    Stock options and the new rules of corporate accountability :
measuring, managing, and rewarding executive performance / by Donald P. Delves.
    p. cm.
    ISBN 0-07-141754-0 (hardcover : alk. paper)
    1. Executives—Salaries, etc.—United States. 2. Employee stock
options—United States. 3. Executives—Salaries, etc.—United
States—Accounting. 4. Employee stock options—United
States—Accounting. 5. Employee fringe benefits—United
States—Accounting. 6. Compensation management—United
States—Accounting. 7. Accounting—Standards—United States. 8.
Corporations—United States—Accounting. I. Title.
    HD4965.5.U6D45 2003
    658.4'07225—dc21   2003007615

1 2 3 4 5 6 7 8 9 0 DOC/DOC 0 9 8 7 6 5 4 3

ISBN 0-07-141754-0

This publication is designed to provide accurate and authoritative information in regard to the subject matter covered. It is sold with the understanding that the publisher is not engaged in rendering legal, accounting, or other professional service. If legal advice or other expert assistance is required, the services of a competent professional person should be sought.

—From a declaration of principles jointly adopted by a committee
of the American Bar Association and a committee of publishers.

McGraw-Hill books are available at special quantity discounts to use as premiums and sales promotions, or for use in corporate training programs. For more information, please write to the Director of Special Sales, Professional Publishing, McGraw-Hill, Two Penn Plaza, New York, NY 10121-2298. Or contact your local bookstore.

 This book is printed on recycled, acid-free paper containing a minimum of 50% recycled, de-inked. fiber.

*Dedicated to
my mentors, Bob and Judith Wright,
and the Wright Institute for Lifelong Learning*

CONTENTS

FOREWORD: A CONVERSATION BETWEEN DON DELVES AND PAUL VOLCKER, FORMER FEDERAL RESERVE CHAIRMAN

When I set out to write this book, my topic was stock options. Specifically, my intent was to explore the much debated issue of expensing stock options. While that remains an essential theme of this book, it is impossible to address stock options without looking at the broader picture. Put another way, stock options are the trees; executive compensation and effective corporate governance are the forest.

After completing this project, I am left with several compelling questions. What can we do differently? How can executive compensation become more balanced and healthier? What changes in corporate governance are necessary to ensure that independent-minded boards are better equipped to design and implement executive compensation packages that are based on performance? How can ownership in a corporation be used as a reward *after* performance is demonstrated instead of as a perk that comes with the job?

This then leads to the ultimate question: what is the purpose of the corporation and how is its success measured? Is the end goal of the corporation to serve its shareholders? If so, then the stock price would be the ultimate benchmark of its success. Or is the purpose of the corporation something more, with shareholders, executives, board members, and employees as integral parts of a greater mission?

These are the questions I had in mind when I spoke with Paul Volcker, former Federal Reserve Chairman (1979 to 1987) and current chairman of the International Accounting Standards Committee (IASC) Foundation, which oversees the International Accounting Standards Board (IASB). Mr. Volcker is also among the 12 members of The Conference Board's Commission on Public Trust and Private Enterprise, which has undertaken an in-depth study of compensation, auditing, and governance issues. He is an outspoken advocate for better corporate governance and more sensible executive compensation.

In our discussion I was pleased to find that Mr. Volcker and I shared many views, particularly the need for a better system of executive compensation and more rational use of stock options. An excerpt from our conversation follows:

Paul Volcker: What I find fascinating is that, even though the market is down, executive compensation has not come down significantly. Stock options, in particular, have continued to be as high, or higher, as in the past.

Don Delves: In recent years, you have been very vocal about your opposition to excessive use of stock options.

Volcker: What I am opposed to are fixed-price stock options for large, broadly held companies. When you talk about stock options, it's easier to think about it the other way around. A private company that's a start-up can do what it wants. It can choose to give away stock in the form of options, largely because it doesn't really have any cash. I would say the same thing applies pretty much for a technological, publicly held company with a large concentrated ownership.

However, when you get to most big, publicly held companies, the stockholder is not in charge. He's at the mercy of what the board says and the board does. The stockholder is pretty far removed in terms of direct decisions. And, except in the most egregious cases, you can get very big stock option grants in a very big company. And it still doesn't have that much dilution for the typical stockholder— not enough that he's going to be charging the barricades over it!

Delves: There are clearly times when stock options make sense and when they do not. For example, with a new company, options are a way to offer stock without really giving ownership, and they are a way to pay people without use of scarce cash. But there is absolutely no way that stock options are the best incentive for every single corporation in America and for every single executive in vast quantities.

Volcker: We never would have had these excesses in executive compensation in my view, except for the growing popularity of stock options. People did not think they were giving away all that much. But when you have the greatest boom in the stock market in all of history, what they thought was very large and generous became grotesque.

Delves: It's gotten to absurd proportions. Another interesting factor is when I assess the value of an option using the Black-Scholes (option valuation) formula. It used to be an option was worth 0.35 times the exercise price. Today it's 0.5 times the exercise price. The reason is because the volatility of the market has gone up. The primary thing that has made an option worth more is the fact that volatility is higher. At the same time that occurred, option grants have gone up 400 to 600 percent. It was a remarkable explosion.

FIGURE I-1

The Good, the Bad, and the Ugly of Stock Options

Good:	Options for start-ups and other cash-strapped companies; options that vest based on performance; options with exercise prices that vary with the market.
OK:	Fixed-price options as part of a mix of performance-based incentives and/or required stock ownership.
Bad:	Fixed-price options for large, established public companies.
Ugly:	Mega grants of fixed-price options to executives of large, established public companies.
Very Ugly:	Mega grants of options to executives of poorly performing companies whose stock price has dropped precipitously.

Volcker: Some people have made the calculation that 80 to 90 percent of the payoff from stock options must be capricious. The problem, however, was that in the midst of a stock market boom, everybody was getting paid off—even if you weren't doing that well. And then it reached truly grotesque proportions when people were getting paid off when the company was going bankrupt! Looking at it in hindsight, and it is partly because of the bull market, you can see just how capricious stock options really were as a reward mechanism. There isn't much relationship between the reward and the effort, the ability, or the contribution.

Delves: You have done a lot of work on board governance, particularly as it relates to executive compensation. How do you get boards to govern better?

Volcker: My favorite corporate governance reform is to have independent directors who make independent judgments and who have responsibility for oversight. That's a starting point. That's the kind of board you ought to have. But it's not going to be effective unless you get some kind of leader of the board who is able to coalesce that discussion. This says to me that the preferred way in an organization is a nonexecutive chairman. Find independent directors, not to be antagonistic, but to have the opportunity to discuss things among themselves, to put things on the agenda, and to demand things be put on the agenda. When something goes wrong and there is a real question about the CEO, then you have some ability to discuss it and take action.

Delves: The other part of executive compensation is the subject of ownership. Why do we feel compelled to give people ownership? Why don't we expect them to earn it? Shouldn't we be structuring compensation systems that say, okay, we're going to give you an interest in the company, but you have to earn it over time? You have to consistently demonstrate and create value in order for this to come to fruition. So if it's an option, it vests based on some kind of long-term, demonstrable performance. It's an option that allows an executive to buy stock at today's price—or even below today's price—but over the next 5, 7, or 10 years. But someone has to consistently create value that is greater than what they are receiving their salary for.

Volcker: In my own thinking I believe this whole idea of equity compensation is overdone. Take this whole idea of paying directors in stock. Should directors who were overseeing the behavior of the company be motivated themselves for the short-term performance of the stock?

Delves: That goes back to the larger point that we focus way too much on stock and stock prices. Some studies show that 75 percent of the movement of the stock has very little to do with what the executives actually do.

Volcker: This is not just a function of stock options, but stock options do exaggerate it. I've told the story many times, but I remember sitting here with a Wall Street business leader. He said, "What can you expect when for 20 years the best business schools have been teaching that all that matters is stock price." I thought about that and came to the conclusion that he was right.

Delves: We were taught to believe that total return to shareholders is the be-all, end-all, and ultimate measure of a company's health and success.

Volcker: But you've got these big public companies, and they aren't issuing any stock. The stock price is irrelevant to their basic financing. Right through this past decade—the greatest bull market in history—what did these companies do? They bought stock. They didn't sell stock. Some individual companies did. But companies as a whole were buying back stock and not issuing stock.

I remember addressing an audience, it was probably during the late 1970s when I was Federal Reserve Chairman, and there was a CEO in the audience. He said, "When it comes right down to it, I don't know why we care that much about stock price. I don't sell stock. I don't go to the market for new capital ever. There are a lot more important things to the company than the day-to-day movement of the stock price."

Delves: If we are not looking at the stock market strictly as a source of equity capital, then that turns everything upside down. We assume the purpose of the company is to serve the shareholders. Yes, they are important as a source of capital. But that capital is used in pursuit of the company's actual purpose: to produce goods and services and sell them in the market.

Volcker: That's right. The purpose of the company is really to provide goods and services at the best possible price, at the highest level of productivity, and in a way that serves society and communities. That is the purpose of the company. The stock is just the way that we get there.

ACKNOWLEDGMENTS

To my wife, Denise, for her consistent belief in me, and whose constant, loving, and sustaining support creates the environment in which I live and work. To my daughter, Lucy, who cheers me on, and is consistently proud of her dad for running a business, writing a book, and doing positive things in the world.

To my father, Gene Delves, on whose shoulders I stand. For his 35 years as an Arthur Andersen partner, which provided me with an example of life as a consultant and what it means to work for a meritocracy, and for his many, invaluable business contacts. To my mother, Sue Delves, whose energetic demeanor and tireless commitment to public service and public speaking have been a great example and inspiration.

To Bob Wright, my mentor and coach, for his inspiring, compelling vision of what's possible, and for leading me to believe I can make a positive difference in the world. To Judith Wright, my spiritual leader and guide, whose dedication to service and her belief that we are all loved deeply and unconditionally have been an inspiration and helped me to expand my vision beyond what I ever thought possible.

To my fellow leaders at the Wright Institute, who coach me, encourage me, give me helpful criticism, and expect the most from me, including Rich and Gertrude Lyons, Mike Zwell, Tom Terry, Angie Calkins, Kathy Schroeder, Barb Burgess, Collin Canright, John Trakselis, Brian Laperriere, Art Silver, Jeff Stitely, Corey Coscioni, Stan Smith, Rob Johnson, James Gustin, Jeff Golden, Kevin McCann, Paul Minnihan, and Marty Goldman.

To John Balkcom, with whom I worked at Sibson and Company, and who encouraged me to pursue stock option reform as a "life's work." To Rich Semmler, who taught me to be a damn good compensation consultant. To Warren Batts, former CEO of Premark, who has coached and encouraged me to speak the truth and understand the perspective of a highly conscientious and concerned board member.

A special thanks to Charles "Chuck" Bowsher, former Controller General of the United States and a member of The Conference Board Commission on Public Trust and Private Enterprise, who appreciated the importance of my message and opened several valuable doors for me.

To the thought leaders who took the time to speak with me and to share their thoughts on compensation in general and stock options in particular. They include John Biggs, immediate past chairman and CEO of the Teachers Insurance and Annuity Association-College Retirement Equities Fund (TIAA-CREF); Graef "Bud" Crystal, former compensation consultant, author, and columnist on executive compensation for Bloomberg.com; John Fiedler, former Chairman and CEO of BorgWarner; Larry Hirsch, Chairman and CEO of Centex Corp.; Gary Hirshberg, Chairman and CEO of Stonyfield Farm; Jim Leisenring, board member of the International Accounting Standards Board (IASB); Jon Najarian, options trader and principal of Mercury Trading and PTI Securities; Ronald Turner, Chairman, President and CEO of Ceridian Corp.; Nobel Laureate and economist Myron Scholes, coauthor of the Black-Scholes methodology for valuing options, and Paul Volcker, former Federal Reserve Chairman, member of the Conference Board Commission, and chairman of the International Accounting Standards Commission Foundation.

To Scott Balutowicz, my associate at the Delves Group, for his valuable research and consistent cheerleading; and to Tricia Jacobs, who assisted with the graphics.

To Ela Booty, who introduced me to my publisher.

To my editor, Kelli Christiansen, for championing this project, for her enthusiasm, and for her valuable editorial guidance.

And to my writer, Tricia Crisafulli, whose brilliance, speed, passion, partnership, and true caring for the message helped shape this book.

(For more information about The Delves Group, please see our Web site at www.delvesgroup.com. To contact the author, send an email to optionsbook@ delvesgroup.com.)

INTRODUCTION: STOCK OPTIONS AND EXECUTIVE COMPENSATION

There are only two reasons to write a book: the first is because you have a particular knowledge or expertise, and the second is because you feel passionately about something. Such are my reasons to write this book.

I have been a consultant in the field of executive compensation for 20 years. I have seen the use of stock options rise as an ever-increasing part of executive compensation. Now we're faced with a watershed event. Nearly a decade after a failed attempt to change the accounting rules, it appears as though Corporate America will be faced with the necessity to expense options. As this book goes to press, the Financial Accounting Standards Board (FASB) and its London-based counterpart, the International Accounting Standards Board (IASB), are drafting and finalizing proposed rules that will require stock options to be expensed.

There has been heated debate over the accounting issue. Companies and consultants have been on both sides of the issue. To weigh in on the debate, I'll state for the record that I am an avid proponent of stock option expensing. Options have a real cost to the company, and they represent something of real value to the recipient. Stock options are a compensation event; they are part of people's pay. Thus stock options are an expense for the company; that's a given. But how that expense is determined and what its implications are for all companies need open and thoughtful debate.

As a Chicago-based compensation consultant and principal of The Delves Group, I've done my share of advising companies on using stock options. I've recommended that companies follow the "standard practice," which for many years meant doling out huge amounts of stock options. I've explained how an accounting expense could be avoided under the current accounting rules (which I'll refer to in this book as the "old" accounting rules). It's part of my job to advise companies on the rules and how they work. I know the intricacies of the loophole and how to avoid running afoul of it.

My stance in favor of option expensing may look like I'm biting the proverbial hand that feeds me. Obviously executives and senior managers have benefited, and in some cases benefited richly from vast quantities of options granted under the "old" rules. The stock price only had to rise modestly in order for these options to pay off handsomely. Executives granted options, for example, with a $10 exercise price when the stock was trading at $10 a share, had to do very little in order to turn a profit. If they kept their feet under their desks and made sure nothing went horribly wrong, they made out handsomely as the stock price rose. Stock price appreciation, over the long term on average, runs 10 to 15 percent per year. Is it good governance or management to provide huge rewards just because things are rolling along? I do not think so.

The truth is all of us who are involved in compensation—whether consultants designing pay packages, board members approving compensation, or executives on the receiving end—are facing a kind of reckoning. We have to move beyond the academic point of option expensing and look at the bigger picture looming in the background. This picture has been clouded with lucrative stock options granted without a clear set of performance criteria, since current or "old" accounting rules made that difficult and unwieldy. Few of us ever stopped to think about the "why" of the compensation packages that increased several hundred percent in the last eight to ten years.

The accounting issue is really an invitation for companies, boards of directors, and the compensation consultants who advise them to become more accountable. Measurement is the key to accountability. As the saying goes what gets measured gets managed. When we account for things, we are held accountable for our actions. Checks and balances are introduced into the system. Compensation is payment for something. Executives are rewarded—and should be rewarded well—for excellence, innovation, and healthy risk-taking to move the company forward. Whatever that compensation looks like—whatever combination of cash compensation, stock, and stock options are offered—there must be commensurate accounting for how that money is earned.

The accounting rule change, therefore, will only be the means to a much better end. The world of executive compensation will be far healthier. CEOs and other top executives will still—and should—make a great deal of money. But the earning of that compensation in accordance with performance standards, goals, and other criteria will be clearer. There will be a more direct link between pay and performance and thus more accountability.

Will stock options disappear? I hardly think so. Nor should they. There is nothing inherently wrong or bad with stock options. The damage is done, however, when huge amounts of stock options—which promise a share of future shareholder wealth—are granted indiscriminately. In the new world of executive compensation, stock options and all other forms of compensation will have to be earned through performance.

Given the decline in the stock market over the past three years, stock options may not be perceived as the bonanza that they once were. There are many companies who have granted stock options in the past, with exercise prices that are far above where the stock is currently traded. Paper fortunes have been amassed and lost. In this environment could the bloom be off the stock-option rose? Perhaps.

Companies must use lucrative rewards to attract and retain talent. Human capital, from the executive office to the sales department to the factory floor, has become increasingly important. But merely granting options "freely" is not going to be the one-size-fits-all solution. For one thing under the proposed ("new") accounting rules, the options will not be free. More importantly companies will need to question if a stock option is the right kind of incentive—with the desired perceived value—to provide to executives and other employees.

Microsoft recently took a bold and revolutionary step in deciding to replace all of its stock options for virtually all of its employees with restricted stock. In so doing, this leader of the technology industry has acknowledged the limited perceived value of options relative to their likely expense and the need to replace them with more highly valued and effective incentives. While the new restricted shares for most employees will vest over five years based only on time with the company, shares granted to the top 600 executives will be based on achieving performance objectives. To truly improve executive compensation, it is critically important that companies do not just blindly replace executive options with time-vesting restricted stock. This will merely replace a gamble with a gift. Future long-term incentives must be based on achieving specific performance goals.

Many others in the broad world of compensation are seeking to do things differently. I have talked with people who have a variety of well-reasoned opinions and points of view. At the end of many chapters you will find questions to consider about stock options and executive compensation, as well as interviews with respected CEOs and other thought leaders. It is my hope through this book to foster a robust debate. The goal is to develop solutions that promote healthier companies and by extension a stronger economy.

PART ONE

The Stock Option Problem

CHAPTER ONE

Dimensions of
the Problem

Over most of the past decade America enjoyed an economic boom in which huge numbers of people benefited. Tremendous wealth was created for shareholders and shared with executives and employees on an unprecedented scale. Nowhere was this explosion in wealth more visible than in executive pay. From 1992 to 2000 median CEO pay increased by 340 percent, and most of that increase was due to the dramatic growth in stock options (see Figure 1-1).

Stock options fueled the rise in median CEO total compensation (salary, annual incentives, and long-term incentives including stock option grants) from $1.8 million in 1992 to $6.1 million in 2000, according to The Conference Board.[1] Mainstream American companies that dedicated 3 to 5 percent of their stock to option grants in the early 1990s increased that allocation to 12 to 15 percent, or more, by 2000. For technology companies, which have a history of giving out large stock option grants to all employees and especially to executives, the percentage is much higher.

Today executive compensation in many companies is out of control and out of balance. Runaway stock option programs for executives have become a corporate epidemic. Born out of the intent to make executives think and act like shareholders, option grants created something entirely different: enormous incentives for executives to think and act like option-holders, with far shorter-term and riskier perspectives than is healthy for most companies.

There are many reasons behind the proliferation of executive stock options, including the prevailing accounting rules that allowed companies to grant large numbers of options as part of compensation packages for essentially no cost. The other and more dangerous reason was ineffective corporate governance. The spectacular explosion in executive pay over the last decade, driven by huge increases in stock option grants, is a symptom of a system with poor checks and balances and ineffective accountability measures.

The massive transfer of wealth and value from shareholders to executives via stock options prompted only a few whimpers from shareholders and boards of directors. It has only been since the sharp decline in the stock market that the investing public and various investor groups have started to cry foul. Only after allegations of manipulation and fraud at Enron, WorldCom, and other companies were disclosed did we start to ask ourselves, how did Corporate America create this mess? Part of the blame can be laid on excessive and escalating stock option grants and an executive pay system with limited and ineffective controls.

The good news, however, is that the ongoing debate over new accounting rules for stock options has opened the door to a fresh perspective on the use of these derivative instruments as part of executive pay. Given its size in monetary terms and its far-reaching impact on the behavior and rewards for executives and employees, compensation deserves a full and intense discussion. Compensation ranks equal in importance to any major capital investment that a company makes and, therefore, should be subject to the same or greater financial rigor. Going forward the key issues of *how* and *how much* to compensate executives, and the impact of those decisions, will be based on a higher level of analysis. In the process Corporate America may not only find a cure for the options epidemic but also adopt far healthier compensation policies and practices.

In this chapter the problem with options and how the prevailing accounting rules were a direct contribution to the problem will be reviewed. Since this book aims to provide a full and thought-provoking discussion of the issues surrounding stock options, the focus will not—and cannot—be on the problem alone. Nor is it wise to see stock options as symptomatic of executive greed. On the contrary greed and the desire to amass "more" are not only inevitable, they are also necessary components of the capitalist system. Execu-

FIGURE 1-1

What Are Employee Stock Options?

Stock Options: The right to purchase a share of stock for a specific price, for a specified period of time. Most options granted to employees give the employee the right to buy the stock at the market price on the day the option is granted. Most options also give that right to employees for a period, or "term," of ten years.

Exercise Price: An option is a right to purchase a share of stock for a specified price. The price is called the exercise price.

Underwater Option: This is an option whose exercise price is higher than the current market price of the stock. Options rarely start out underwater. They start out "at the money," meaning that the exercise is equal to the market price. If the stock price drops below the exercise price after it is granted, then the option is "underwater" and as such is not worth much.

In the Money Options: An option is "in the money" when the market price is higher than the exercise price. This is good because you can exercise the option and buy the stock for less than you can sell it for in the stock market.

Option Dilution: When earnings per share is calculated, net income is divided by the total number of outstanding shares of stock. When stock options are granted, and especially when those options are "in the money," the number of new shares used in calculating "fully diluted" earnings per share is increased to reflect the potential net number of new shares that would be issued if all options were exercised. This reduces or "dilutes" the earnings-per-share number.

Black-Scholes Option Pricing Model: This is a statistical formula developed in 1973 by Fischer Black and Myron Scholes to estimate the market value of a publicly traded stock option. This model and variations of this model are used every day to determine prices for options traded on the public exchanges.

Fair Market Value: The value of a stock or option if it were traded on the open market.

Overhang: The percentage of the company's stock that is devoted to options. The calculation is the number of options granted and outstanding, plus the number of shares reserved for future grants divided by the number of shares outstanding.

Restricted Shares: These are shares of stock granted to an employee. While they are officially owned by the employee (who gets dividends and can vote the shares), they have restrictions on them. The restrictions make it so the share of stock may not be sold or transferred (given) to anyone else. Usually the restricted shares vest over time. When the restricted shares vest, the restrictions lapse and the shares can then be sold if the employee wishes. If the employee leaves the company before the shares vest and the restrictions lapse, he or she loses all rights to the shares.

tive compensation is a principal tool of the capitalist system used to drive and channel individual desires toward prescribed ends.

The growing chorus of dissent among shareholder groups and regulators about stock options in particular and executive compensation in general will also be addressed in this chapter. But that is not where the reform needs to focus. The spotlight should rest squarely on corporate management and their boards of directors. Board members in particular must break out of the status quo for executive compensation and look beyond competitive practice to consider their own policies on pay and performance. Today and in the future board members are the crucial players in the stock options game—and on the broader playing field of executive compensation.

THE PROBLEM WITH OPTIONS

Executive stock options are a problem for two reasons. First companies have granted too many of them. Second they are ineffective incentives and rewards at most companies. This has been exacerbated by accounting rules that contributed directly to the untenable mess that all of us involved in executive compensation, including executives, board members, and compensation consultants, must address.

Let's look at the facts. Under current accounting a very narrow definition of a derivative security—specifically an at-the-money call option granted to an executive or other employee—receives a very special accounting treatment. These options have no expense whatsoever associated with them, no matter how many are exercised and no matter how much money executives make from them. Through this strange but very tempting little loophole, truckloads of options grants have been delivered to executives with no expense to the companies granting them. Because of this same loophole, hundreds of billions of dollars of shareholder value have been transferred to executives with virtually no controls or limitations. But this is only part of the story.

More importantly because of this loophole, approximately 95 percent of public companies pay their executives in *exactly* the same way, using *exactly* the same specific derivative security. And they have blindly granted them in substantial and ever-increasing numbers. I refuse to believe that large quantities of at-the-money call options are the *best* incentive for virtually *every* public company. There is no way that if every company in America started with a blank sheet of paper, virtually all of them would simultaneously conclude that this particular form of incentive is precisely the best one for them. That is absurd.

This might not be a problem if we knew that options were (A) an effective incentive and (B) a cost-effective way to deliver that incentive, but we do not. Because there is no expense, companies have never been forced to make this determination. They just keep granting these narrowly defined derivative securities in increasingly larger quantities, as illustrated in Figure 1-2. All the while 10 to 15 percent or more of the increase in value of the entire stock market is being "transferred" from the pockets of shareholders into the pockets of employees—and mostly into the pockets of executives.

As I will discuss in the latter chapters, options are not effective as incentives for a variety of reasons (see Chapters 6 and 7). The point is that increasingly larger option grants by virtually all companies are likely a misuse of corporate resources. In a few companies options have contributed to some highly dysfunctional and overly risky behavior. In the majority of companies, they have been

FIGURE 1-2

Executive Compensation Growth

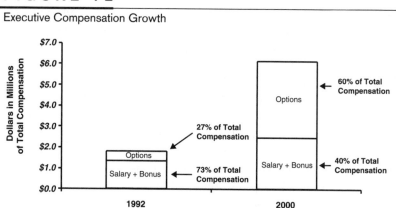

In 1992 the median compensation paid to CEOs was $1.8 million. Of this median compensation 27% was paid in the form of stock options. By 2000 the median compensation increased to $6.1 million with stock options contributing 60% of the total compensation.

Source: The Conference Board on Public Trust and Private Enterprise

ineffective incentives to encourage and reward meaningful and sustainable corporate performance.

Clearly many steps must be taken by companies and their boards, including examining the expensing issue, weighing the pros and cons of stock options, exploring alternative forms of incentives, and improving board governance over executive compensation. Before considering these issues in later chapters of the book, it is important to discuss the dimensions of the problem a bit further.

THE CURRENT SITUATION

Despite the decline in corporate performance since 2000, total executive compensation packages have remained very generous, particularly when it comes to stock options, according to an April 2002 *Wall Street Journal* special report. Total direct compensation for CEOs fell 0.9 percent; the first downturn since the newspaper began tracking this data in 1989.[2] Total direct compensation includes salary, bonus, restricted stock value at the time of the grant, gains from exercising options, and other long-term incentive payouts.

While this reported compensation has declined slightly, many executives have more than made up for any drop in cash compensation with substantial additional stock option grants. According to the *Journal* article, top executives of 111 of the 350 firms surveyed received *mega* option grants in 2001, up from 85 in 2000. A mega grant has a face value of at least eight times an individual's salary and bonus. (The face value is the number of options granted times the exercise price per option.)

As long as options grants were "free" with no required expense, executive compensation never really declined. Even in a bad year, when CEO salary and bonuses decreased due to poor corporate performance, companies made up the difference with even larger option grants. For example, a CEO who received a $900,000 base salary and a $500,000 bonus also received a mega grant of options on $11.2 million in stock. This means the CEO has been given the right to the increase in value on $11.2 million in stock for the next 10 years. If the company's shares go up only 10 percent in value, when he exercises his options from the mega grant, he will make $1.12 million. This profit would be in addition to the options he normally receives annually on $2 million to $3 million in stock.

EXECUTIVE WEALTH AND THE POSITIVE POWER OF GREED

News stories have illustrated the magnitude of the wealth that executives can reap through the receipt of stock options. In the *New York Times Magazine* article "Heads I Win, Tails I Win," Roger Lowenstein examined the pay of the top executive of SBC Communications, a company he chose "for its unspectacular qualities."[3] Lowenstein wrote: "It is profitable and professionally managed, and its CEO is well regarded in his industry. Like many CEOs he pursued a bold growth strategy for much of the 90's, had some good early years and more recently gave back much of his gains. In the last three years, his stock has fallen 27 percent—more than either the Standard & Poor's 500 or the stock of his Baby Bell peers." Nonetheless CEO Edward E. Whitacre, Jr., received the "largest pay package of his career—one with a present value of $82 million," Lowenstein wrote. Stock options are the backbone of Whitacre's compensation package, which included a grant of 3.6 million options with an estimated value of $61 million.

It comes as no surprise that CEOs and top executives want to be rewarded for their efforts—and the greater the results, the greater the reward. Greed is a natural force that drives capitalism. But just like steam power and electricity, which have to be harnessed and directed with capacitors and resistors in order to be used productively, so do the innate desires for bigger, better, and more. Executive compensation policies must provide the methods and systems to effectively harness and focus these powerful forces that drive companies and, in fact, the entire U.S. economy. Greed itself is not the problem. The fault lies with the lack of limits and effective controls to manage it.

Acknowledging the basic human desire to acquire and amass more, companies can motivate executives and employees to perform better, produce high-quality sustainable results, and do more for the good of the company and themselves. Many companies, however, have not effectively harnessed the power of greed and have largely given in to this executive appetite.

As Federal Reserve Board Chairman Alan Greenspan observed in his July 2002 testimony on monetary policy to Congress, "Why did corporate governance checks and balances that served us reasonably well in the past break down? At the root was the rapid enlargement of stock market capitalization in the latter part of the 1990s that arguably engendered an outsized increase in opportunities for avarice. An infectious greed seemed to grip much of our business community. Our historical guardians of financial information were overwhelmed. Too many corporate executives sought ways to 'harvest' some of those stock market gains.

"As a result, the highly desirable spread of shareholding and options among business managers perversely created incentives to artificially inflate reported earnings in order to keep stock prices high and strong," Greenspan said.

Clearly Corporate America has lacked the appropriate checks, balances, and guidelines on its executive compensation system. The result has been, to use Greenspan's infamous phrase, "irrational exuberance" among companies and top executives to reap short-term wealth instead of focusing on sustained performance and enduring results.

STOCK OPTIONS AND CORPORATE CULTURE

When stock options—particularly large amounts of them—are offered to executives as incentives, the corporate culture is potentially impacted. While stock options do not create the corporate culture of high-risk behavior, they do contribute to it. In a corporate environment in which there is the potential to engage in high-risk behaviors, options provide a lucrative reward. As stock options and other incentives impact executive and management behavior, they can directly influence the types of risks that a company takes on.

The world does not need one more rehashing of the Enron debacle. The demise of this high-flying, high-risk energy company, which helped bring down a once revered accounting firm, has filled business- and front-page headlines. While Enron's collapse has focused attention on the issuance of misleading financial statements, there is also the issue of the amount of stock options Enron granted. From 1996 to 2000, according to Congressional statements, the company issued nearly $600 million in stock options.

It is too simplistic to state that stock options caused the downfall of Enron, whose falsified financial books in a roaring bull market helped the stock price rise to about $90 a share in mid-2000. Yet looking back at the unraveling of Enron, there is no doubt stock options were a powerful incentive that helped to reinforce a high-risk corporate culture. Interestingly option incentives may have been well matched to the high-risk, high-reward behavior of Enron's executives. Options were quite effective at reinforcing exactly the type of behavior the company espoused. On the other hand it is obvious in retrospect that Enron should have had an incentive system placing controls and limits on its executives' high-risk behavior and holding them accountable to long-term, sustainable results.

For individuals who are prone to high-risk behaviors or who become swept up in a culture that embraces risk, stock options that pay off when the stock price goes up (or is inflated) provide an almost irresistible temptation. Moreover the spread of stock options among the corporate ranks can make the effects of these incentives even more pervasive. If I work at a company that overlooks or even encourages high-risk behavior, will I care what the top executives do to enrich themselves with their "ba-zillion" options if I have a "half ba-zillion"? Will I risk my own chance for wealth in order to say something?

SHAREHOLDER ACTIVISM

The tide, however, is turning. Shareholders, regulators, Wall Street, and many boards are turning an attentive eye toward executive compensation practices and stock option grants. While it ultimately rests with company management and their boards of directors to make informed decisions and take decisive actions on executive pay, many forces are pressing for change.

Shareholder activists, including groups who have long pressed for increased board independence, have indicated their growing concern over escalating executive pay and option grants. For example the California Public Employees' Retirement Systems (CalPERS), which has a long history of campaigning for shareholder rights and corporate governance issues, recently took a stance on executive compensation. In a June 2002 memorandum entitled "Market Report—Corporate Governance," CalPERS noted, "one element that seems to be lacking is significant involvement by shareowners in the compensation process. While owners do play a role in approving some portions of compensation plans, they are rarely involved in compensation policy related issues, and in our experience rarely consulted for input on compensation in general. A concerted effort by owners to voice their opinion regarding key policy issues related to compensation could play a very positive role in helping to curb abusive pay packages, but also in encouraging model compensation design."[4]

Notably CalPERS did not recommend an expense for stock options. We can only assume this reflects California's large base of technology companies, which almost unanimously oppose stock option expensing.

Similarly the Teachers Insurance and Annuity Association— College Retirement Equities Fund (TIAA–CREF) has drafted its "five fundamental principles of compensation governance," which it applies as "new concepts of compensation are introduced, and in voting proxies related to compensation and to board composition."

The State of Wisconsin Investment Board (SWIB) took on the issue of corporate governance and executive compensation with a September 2002 conference that brought together institutional shareholders, public policymakers, and corporate leaders. Findings at the conference included changes in the way stock options are typically granted; specifically advocating a longer vesting period and requiring that once options were exercised, the stock should be held for a minimum of one to two years. The group also believed one of the primary reasons for excessive executive compensation was the lack of good succession planning by companies and their boards.

The chorus of criticism on the issue of executive compensation has widened to include government and public officials. Former New York Federal Reserve President William J. McDonough, who was regarded as the second most powerful person at the Fed behind Chairman Alan Greenspan, called on U.S. corporate executives to take pay cuts. In his speech at a September 11, 2002, one-year anniversary event in New York, he noted, "Beginning with the strongest companies, CEOs and their boards should simply reach the conclusion that executive pay is excessive and adjust it to more reasonable and justifiable levels."

McDonough, who is now Chair of the Public Company Accounting Oversight Board, called the rise in executive pay—which studies show has gone from 42 to more than 400 times that of the average production worker in the past 20 years—"terribly bad social policy and perhaps even bad morals." This is an unusually harsh and pointed comment to come from the Federal Reserve.

At the May 2003 Kellogg School of Management corporate governance conference, I was impressed and encouraged by the number of Fortune 100 board members who expressed their concern over the magnitude of executive compensation, and the fact that stock option grants have gotten "out of control." The general consensus was that the need for better governance of executive compensation runs a close second in importance behind the need for improved financial and auditing controls. What's important is that this core power base of Corporate America clearly acknowledges that the executive compensation system has serious flaws. There is a clear call for dramatically changing the way we think about and structure executive compensation.

THE SPECTER OF GOVERNMENT REGULATIONS

Tough talk in the public and governmental sectors should sound a warning to companies and raise the specter of additional regulations. Quite frankly this is the last thing that companies need, particularly in the wake of the Sarbanes-Oxley Act of 2002, which was created to "protect investors by improving the accuracy and reliability of corporate disclosures." The Sarbanes-Oxley Act is the most important and sweeping securities legislation since the 1930s. Among a host of other provisions, it requires that CEOs and CFOs sign off on their financial statements, making a public declaration that the facts and figures are legitimate and verified. This particular requirement was passed because the former CEO and CFO of Enron, in testimony to Congress, stated that they could not be responsible for their own financial statements, and that their auditors were to blame. This so deeply offended members of Congress that they didn't want a top executive to ever be able to say that again. The Act also includes an array of provisions requiring better auditing and oversight by boards.

At one point during the Senate debate on Sarbanes-Oxley, two senators who have championed stock-option accounting reform—Sens. Carl Levin (D-Mich) and John McCain (R-Ariz)—attempted to offer amendments to address this issue. The Levin amendment would have directed the FASB to review and take "appropriate" actions on stock option accounting within a year. The McCain amendment would have directed the FASB to require companies to treat stock option compensation as an expense on their financial statements. In the end, however, both amendments were objected to, neither was voted on, and no provision in the final Sarbanes-Oxley law addressed stock options.

Given the blatant examples, as described in a recent speech by former Federal Reserve Chairman Paul Volcker, of corporate "malfeasance, misfeasance, and nonfeasance," we can hardly blame Congress for passing Sarbanes-Oxley. However given the examples of excess and poorly designed corporate pay, it is not out of the realm of possibility that regulators would seek to impose some standard or measures on corporate compensation. After all it happened in 1994 with the million-dollar pay cap and could easily happen again. Corporate America doesn't need regulations on executive pay. It needs more proactive boards of directors, who see the big picture, ask tough and probing questions, and take on the role of the ultimate authority and "accountability cop."

Proactive steps taken by companies to expense stock options and to re-evaluate the composition of their executive compensation packages will be rewarded with greater shareholder confidence. Just as Congress looked for assurance of financial results in the form of CEO-certified financial statements, investors will look most favorably on companies with innovative and balanced executive compensation packages. And, just as companies are rewarded by watchdog groups and other organizations for being "family friendly" or having a diverse workforce, soon corporations will be ranked by their fairness and balance in executive compensation, including the judicious use of stock options. In fact, longtime shareholder activist Nell Minow has formed a new organization, The Corporate Library, dedicated to providing in-depth information on and evaluation of corporate performance and governance. The Corporate Library has chosen effective executive compensation as its primary area of focus and is developing a thorough rating system for evaluating the quality, effectiveness, and fairness of companies' executive pay programs.

In the words of former SEC Chairman Arthur Levitt, quoted in a September 2002 *Fortune* magazine article, "You've got a totally disaffected individual investor community, and they're angry. They're going to differentiate between companies that stand with them and companies that don't."[5]

The obvious remedy to quell the fears of shareholders and regulators is to have boards of directors do what they are supposed to do: act with independence and authority to provide the proper oversight to companies. Proactive and empowered boards of directors must oversee and enact greater accountability and help engender a healthier corporate environment for the long term. In this context the ongoing debate over proposed accounting rules that would require stock option expensing is extremely timely.

A SEA CHANGE FOR OPTIONS AND EXECUTIVE COMPENSATION

As will be discussed in Chapter 3, there has already been a significant change among many companies with regard to stock option expensing. Companies that have publicly announced expensing stock options include Coca-Cola Company, Bank One, The Washington Post, and Amazon.com. While expensing stock options is a very healthy first step, the journey toward healthier executive compensation in the United States does not end there. In time I believe companies will adopt a more balanced approach to executive compensation, with the right blend of salary, bonuses, stock options, performance-based options, performance-based restricted stock, and stock ownership. Specific elements of compensation plans and incentives are discussed later in the book. For now the important word to consider is "balanced," not only in the components of the compensation itself but also in the rationale behind it.

BOARD RESPONSIBILITY

The responsibility for executive compensation oversight falls clearly on the board of directors. Until very recently, however, boards have not asked the tough questions beyond ascertaining if the company's compensation is in line with "common industry practices." They have not adequately considered the impact of incentives on the company's risk profile and the way decisions are made by top executives. But companies and their boards are waking up to this idea, albeit slowly.

Because of the excesses of the past, the criticism of boards has been pervasive but also deserved. Articles in the press have detailed the director networks that appear to confirm and even condone the "you sit on my board and I'll sit on yours" relationships. In his *New York Times Magazine* article on SBC Communications, Roger Lowenstein noted that many board members have been close to CEO Whitacre and "have been endorsing his pay for a long time. He also has been endorsing theirs." Lowenstein reported that two of SBC's "nominally independent directors"—August A. Busch III of Anheuser-Busch and Charles Knight of Emerson Electric—run companies for which Whitacre is a director. "Most of the other 18 directors have either served with Whitacre for at least 10 years or were directors of companies that Whitacre acquired."

I do not mean to single out Mr. Whitacre nor indicate that his board is particularly unusual. (He just happened to have an article written about him.) What's important is that the structure of the SBC board reflects common practice among America's corporate boards.

Understandably corporations want harmonious relationships between board members and top management. A hostile board, as seen in the midst of corporate takeovers and other "raider" activity, is disruptive and potentially damaging to the company. But a board that is truly independent and seeks to act in the best interests of shareholders and the company will be an asset to the corporation, not a detriment. For that to happen boards must be empowered and encouraged to take an in-depth look at executive compensation, going beyond the typical "standard industry practice." Board members should be independently advised to help promote objectivity and fairness.

In the almost 20 years that I have been advising corporate boards on executive pay, I have seen far too few examples of meaningful, insightful analysis of compensation packages. As long as compensation packages aren't significantly different from what other companies are doing then the board can rest assured that it has adequately done its duty.

This is reminiscent of the advice my mother used to give me when I wanted to do something that "all the other kids were doing." "Well," my mother would say, "if all the other children were jumping off a cliff, would you do it too?"

Corporate boards have been all too willing to follow the Pied Piper of competitive practice instead of taking a long, hard look at their own practices. The question, "Will we stand out too much for what we are doing?" is no longer sufficient in determining the size and scope of executive compensation. Rather the issue of standing out should apply in a very positive way to the amount of quality oversight and study given to the issue of executive compensation and corporate governance.

Companies and their boards must wake up to the fact that options, on their own, do not provide balanced incentives. Options only reward individuals when the stock price goes up, without much disincentive to keep the stock from going down. As long as the stock price goes up briefly, options can conceivably be exercised, even if the stock price declines months or even weeks later.

A shift in strategy to a more balanced, realistic, and healthy approach to compensation (as I will discuss in Chapters 8 and 9) does not need to dilute executive pay. If anything there will still be opportunities for executives, over the long term, to be fairly and even richly rewarded for their efforts to develop and execute plans for solid and sustainable growth at their companies.

A change in attitude and behavior will be necessary for both board members and top executives. Boards have been reluctant to ask the tough questions, particularly about compensation, for fear of upsetting management. Management also does not want to subject itself to a high degree of self-examination. None of us really likes accountability. Like bad-tasting medicine we know it's good for us but we will seek it out only when absolutely necessary, and then only in the absolutely necessary doses.

The accountability issue may make for some uncomfortable discussions between board members and senior executives. While the discussion of expectations and performance are difficult enough between employer and subordinate, between board members and CEOs it seems almost offensive. Boards will also have to address the struggle of holding executives accountable and the fear that they will leave. Whether you're running General Motors or the local sandwich shop, there is always the underlying concern that your employees will leave if you hold them too accountable. Or if you demand more of them, your employees will demand more pay or perks. At the top executive level, it is no different. In fact given the supposed scarcity of top executive talent, the situation is much worse. Companies are often so worried about people leaving, they are willing to bribe and seduce them with almost anything to keep them. "Free" stock options were an easy inducement.

It is not enough to adopt accounting standards without addressing executive accountability standards. The goal of this book is to provide companies, their boards, and all other parties involved in executive compensation with the right questions that they should be considering. It is neither helpful nor healthy to dwell exclusively on the problems and excesses of the past. With a full realization of the situation now facing companies, board members must take up the cause of change. To do so they must be prepared to ask the right questions so that they can obtain the right answers.

WHAT DO YOU THINK?

- What are the purpose and objectives of our executive compensation program?

  What values, behaviors, and results are we trying to instill and motivate?

  What messages are we sending?
- What is the total cost of our executive compensation program?

  This is not just the total accounting expense, even with the proper expense for options.

  The analysis must incorporate the actual and expected economic cost of the program over a multiyear period, and under a variety of performance scenarios.
- What are we getting in return for our investment in executive compensation?

  Are the expectations commensurate with the rewards?
- Does our executive pay program provide the right trade-off between risks and rewards, reflecting the values, culture and risk profile of our company?

CHAPTER TWO

The Sources of
the Problem

The spirit of capitalism is alive and well in Corporate America. Darwinian economies, governed by the basic laws of supply and demand, vastly favor the strong while eliminating the weak and inefficient. Not only do the strong survive in a capitalist economy, they are also richly rewarded. But it doesn't end there. In fact what is great about capitalism is that it has its own accountability built in, just like Darwinian theory does.

Capitalism brings with it its own rewards and consequences. When the system is working at its best—well-governed by good legal and accounting systems—it can drive people to perform to their highest and best use. However when the controls break down, our natural desires and competitiveness wrestle with greed, and our darker nature wins out. We must constantly monitor the controls to keep the natural force of capitalism moving toward a higher purpose. Well-designed executive compensation is part of the accountability system that keeps us focused and on track.

BRIEF HISTORY OF COMPENSATION

Executive compensation did not become an issue until the turn of the last century when the industrial revolution created enterprises like General Electric, founded in 1892; U.S. Steel, 1901; and International Harvester, 1902. These corporations were so vast and required investment from so many sources that they could no longer be managed by their owners. Thus a new class of professional—the corporate manager—was created. While this was an efficient way to run an organization, it did introduce a new problem: how to establish compensation for managers who had authority and control but not ownership. If these nonowner managers had control over their own compensation, there would be an inherent conflict of interest that could easily lead to excessive pay. Companies then developed compensation plans, bonuses, and profit-sharing formulas intended to create rational ways of paying people for doing what was in the best interest of the owners.

Excessive executive compensation did not become a public issue until the late 1920s when a magazine disclosed that Eugene G. Grace, president of Bethlehem Steel, was paid a salary of $12,000 and a bonus of $1,623,753 in 1929. The disclosure of Grace's substantial pay—which compared to a "good" management salary in those days of $1000 a year—and the subsequent public outrage was one of many factors that contributed to the founding of the Securities and Exchange Commission (SEC). One of the SEC's first requirements was for disclosure of executive pay.

Bonuses and profit sharing became common in the teens and the 1920s, followed by a rise in fixed compensation in the 1930s. From 1939 until 1950 executive pay went up only by a third while at the same time worker pay doubled. This was due to the rise of labor unions, the New Deal legislation, the shortage of labor due to World War II, and the post-war release of controls placed on prices and wages.

Another major influence on the way executive compensation was delivered in the 1940s and 1950s was a graduated income-tax structure that topped out at a remarkable 91 percent for the highest income levels. While this level of taxation did not affect most Americans, senior executives were affected and actively sought ways to avoid it.

High income-tax rates led to the development of many types of noncash compensation, including deferred compensation, thrift plans, stock options, group life and split-dollar insurance, and medical and hospitalization plans. In 1950 the Revenue Act created the "restricted stock option," which shielded gains at exercise from taxes until the shares were sold. Once the shares were sold a capital gains tax rate of 25 percent applied. The modern era of compensation was under way. Despite a variety of changes in the tax code, options and other forms of noncash and long-term incentives continued to gain in popularity, usage, and size. The modern history of compensation from the 1950s and into the 1990s will be explored later in this chapter.

CULTURAL PHENOMENA

Before we delve into our understanding of modern compensation practices, we must look more deeply into the uniquely American phenomenon of extremely high executive compensation and the wide disparities in pay between managers and workers. Just as the power of capitalism seems to be stronger and more pronounced in America than anywhere else in the world, so does the propensity to pay certain people—whether executives, movie stars, or sports figures—exceptional amounts of money.

American culture, like no other, is imbued with the value and the rewards of work. This can be traced back to the practical sayings of statesman and philosopher Benjamin Franklin. His philosophy—such as the often quoted "time is money"—espoused not only work and wealth, but also the downfall brought on by idleness. The concepts that work is good and the fruits of one's labors are "blessings" stem from a system of beliefs celebrating the "spirit of capitalism." Working, earning, and amassing are not just God-given rights; they are evidence of heavenly benediction.

The Protestant Ethic in America

In his epic *The Protestant Ethic and the Spirit of Capitalism*, first published in 1904, Max Weber, a founding father of modern sociology, states that the Protestant ethic encouraged the development of capitalism in the West. Under this system of beliefs, not only was the pursuit of wealth encouraged, it was sanctified. While some people today may not see a direct link between business and religion, Weber saw strong correlations that can be carried through to the present time.

"The capitalistic economy of the present day is an immense cosmos into which the individual is born, and which presents itself to him, at least as an individual, as an unalterable order of things in which he must live. It forces the individual, in so far as he is involved in the system of market relationships, to conform to capitalistic rules of action. The manufacturer who in the long run acts counter to these norms, will just as inevitably be eliminated from the economic scene as the worker who cannot or will not adapt himself to them will be thrown into the streets without a job," Weber wrote.

"Thus the capitalism of today, which has come to dominate economic life, educates and selects the economic subjects which it needs through a process of economic survival of the fittest."

Neither Weber, nor Franklin whom he quotes, had any trouble with the idea of the capitalistic nature of humankind. In their eyes we were put on Earth to work and be rewarded. Even the austere Pilgrims did not shy away from amassing land and fattening up the cattle. Indeed, it was all about harvesting the fruits of the earth over which humankind had been given dominion. But there was an even bigger belief behind the capitalistic system. The Protestant ethic saw financial and creature comforts in this life as evidence of having been "blessed," and thus being a likely candidate for a heavenly reward.

The connection between having the "good life" on Earth and being destined for a reward in the afterlife was a direct result of the Protestant Reformation. Rejecting the Vatican's views that the Church and its priests were the designated intermediaries between God and humankind, the Protestant movement averred that a direct relationship was possible. But how to distinguish between those who were "chosen" and therefore predestined for heaven (under a Calvinist view) and those who were not? Early American settlers found proof in the appearance of abundance and fruitfulness. Those who were well-off were given the front pews of the New England churches—and presumably a first-class ticket to heaven.

Over the years the belief that abundance is direct evidence of a heavenly benediction has come to confirm—or at least add a spiritual veneer to—America's unbridled thirst for wealth and well-being. In fact the Protestant ethic is a strong theme that runs unspoken but well understood in our uniquely American system of work and meritocracy.

The "Star" CEO

Another fundamental underpinning of American culture at work is the near deification of the "star" CEO. Their names are synonymous with the companies they led, such as Chrysler's Lee Iacocca, IBM's Lou Gerstner, AT&T's Michael Armstrong, and Coca-Cola's Roberto Goizueta. Despite the disclosure of his ultra-generous retirement package, ex-GE CEO Jack Welch is revered for his tough, no-nonsense stance. Even when they are not well liked, they earn a respect borne of their sheer might, determination, and, of course, their winner status. They are what *Harvard Business Review* calls the "star" CEOs.

Given the Protestant ethic that underscores our association of the spiritual and the economic, there's little surprise that Rakesh Khurana, an assistant professor of organizational behavior at Harvard Business School, uses religious terminology in describing the attributes of the "star" CEO.

"When people describe the qualities that enable a CEO to lead, the word they use most often is 'charisma.' ... Nevertheless, charisma remains as difficult to define as art or love. Few who advocate it are able to convey what they mean by the term. Fewer still are aware that the concept is borrowed from Christianity," Khurana writes. [6]

As Khurana explains, in the New Testament Saint Paul writes of the "charisms," or gifts of the Holy Spirit that Christians may possess. Those gifted with charisma were thought to be good leaders. While the meaning of charisma has changed over time, there is still a sense of admiration for those chosen few considered to have unique inspirational powers.

Believing their CEO (or incoming CEO) to be a star, companies react in a predictable manner. They seek to reward this top talent lavishly to show appreciation and, more importantly, to keep them from going someplace else. This fundamental belief has driven executive compensation to the outrageous highs we've seen in recent years, which, despite the drop in corporate performance and stock prices, continues today. Companies pin their hopes on messianic CEOs to save the firm, turn around performance, and make all things right. When CEOs do, they are rewarded with a king's ransom in salary, bonuses, and stock options. Even when they cannot perform financial miracles—perhaps because of deteriorating economic conditions, heightened competition, or because they're merely mortal—they are often given the benefit of the doubt and even more financial rewards to make sure they are "properly motivated."

The charisma or star quality of CEOs has been a driving force in the recruitment and hiring of top CEOs. They are sought out not only for their own merits, but also because of their association with other deified executives. In the *Harvard Business Review* article Khurana detailed the hiring of John Trani as CEO of tool and hardware manufacturer Stanley Works. Asked why Trani was selected, the factor mentioned the most by Stanley board members was that he had worked for GE's Welch. As Khurana wrote, "Several directors discussed GE's track record in developing executives. All of them pointed to other former GE executives who were now leading U.S. companies. . . . Not one of the directors made any explicit connection between Trani's experiences at GE and the problems facing Stanley. In their eyes Trani had been imbued with charisma simply through his association with GE and Welch."

Corporations rise to prominence, however, based on the strength of their organizations, not because of one individual acting alone. This flies in the face of the myth of the outside CEO who, it is hoped, can single-handedly restructure, redirect, revitalize, and rescue the company. All companies are a conglomeration of people and their talents. They are systems allowing individuals to interact in the creation of products and services and then selling and delivering them to the marketplace. A talented CEO can rally the troops and march on to victory in the marketplace. But the success of a CEO will depend largely upon the cooperation he or she receives from within the organization and from the existing strength of the organization itself. A case in point: Disney CEO Michael Eisner. Yes he's done a great job leading Disney. And he had a lot to work with, including the foundational values of the company, its products and properties, and the solid-gold Disney name.

The myth of the star CEO is also challenged in the book *Built to Last: Successful Habits of Visionary Companies*, which argues that while leaders may come and go, the power of the organization remains. "The key point is that a visionary company is an organization—an institution. *All* individual leaders, no matter how charismatic or visionary, eventually die; and all visionary products and services—all 'great ideas'—eventually become obsolete. Indeed entire markets can become obsolete and disappear. Yet visionary *companies* prosper over long periods of time, through multiple product life cycles and multiple generations of active leaders."

When a powerful and charismatic leader takes the helm, however, the tendency is to forget the legacy and over time give all the credit—or sometimes all the blame—for what transpires to the incoming CEO. Such is the legend that surrounded Welch, who became CEO of GE in 1981. "To read the myriad articles on Welch's revolution, we might be tempted to picture him as a savior riding on a white horse to rescue a severely troubled company that had not changed significantly since the invention of electricity," state *Built to Last* authors James C. Collins and Jerry I. Porras, who undertook a six-year research project of "visionary companies."

Welch, however, was an insider, having spent 20 consecutive years at GE before becoming CEO. Further, his immediate predecessor, Reginald Jones, retired as "the most admired business leader in America." As the book also notes, in terms of profit growth, return on equity, return on sales, and return on assets, GE performed as well under Jones's eight-year tenure as during Welch's first eight years.

Clearly a talented and tough CEO like Welch was no more solely responsible for the success of GE than George W. Bush (or any one president or presidential candidate before him) is responsible for the United States being the No. 1 Superpower. Welch was the latest in a succession of strong CEOs at GE, which speaks volumes about the quality of the leadership and the grooming of executives at the company.

When companies look to a corporate savior—often an outsider brought in as a combination hired gun and miracle worker—the serious problem of displaced responsibility can result. Everyone, from the board of directors through the ranks of employees, credits the CEO when things go well. When things go badly they point fingers and avoid responsibility. Inevitably this behavior leads companies to look externally for the next solution: another star CEO to recruit and retain.

A far healthier corporate environment is created when the CEO—even one with charisma—recognizes the power of the organization. Bank One CEO Jamie Dimon fits this description. From my own experiences working with Bank One as well as stories related by executives there, Dimon continually challenges and empowers employees with a straightforward message. "If you see something wrong in the organization and just complain about it, then you are part of the problem. If you do not speak up to solve that problem and bring it to someone's attention, you are only making things worse. And if you have spoken up and you're getting resistance or getting in trouble, or if you feel you are not being heard, then send me an e-mail. I will respond."

As CEO, Dimon has made changes in the top executive tier, and eliminated many perks and giveaway bonuses, including rejecting a $2 million bonus guaranteed in his contract because he felt that the company's performance did not warrant it. Under his leadership Bank One's compensation system is based far more on performance. Bank One was also among the first three companies to announce in 2002 that it would elect to expense options.

In many corporations, however, the cult of the CEO remains strong. This reinforces the belief that companies must pay *anything* to attract and retain superstar leaders. Since stock options have been free under current accounting, they became the currency of choice for executive compensation. Options became the "magic dust" needed to attract and retain the star CEO and his or her executive team.

Overall there are some powerful cultural forces at work here. First there is the Protestant ethic that says vast wealth is evidence of heavenly benediction—a concept that drives the United States more than other countries. The second is the uniquely American cult of the deified CEO and his entourage, making them worthy of vast sums of money to attract and retain them.

That brings us to the next point: to provide large, lucrative rewards to executive talent, companies have increasingly used the stock option. In fact it has become the primary means to deliver wealth to CEOs and other executives. To understand this phenomenon we need to consider the recent history of executive compensation and in particular stock options.

MODERN HISTORY OF COMPENSATION

Stock options became a common form of executive compensation starting in the 1950s, and gained fairly wide acceptance among public companies in the 1960s. Like the 1990s, the 1960s saw a huge explosion in technology, which fueled tremendous economic growth and a sense of unbounded potential. Recall that the 1960s included the development of the mainframe computer, color television, advancements in space travel, nuclear power, and telecommunications on a global scale. Everyone wanted to participate in this expansion. Stock options were then—as they would be in the 1990s—a convenient and cost-effective way to share wealth-creation opportunities with executives.

The economic expansion of the 1960s, unfortunately, was followed by a decade in which the stock market experienced virtually no growth. The 1970s were marked by oil embargoes and high unemployment. It was a time of the dreaded "stag-flation," caused by a stagnant economy and high inflation. There was low confidence in the capital markets and in the U.S. dollar.

With the stock market flat in the 1970s, stock options went out of favor since they delivered little value to executives. Instead there was a shift to "long-term performance plans," which included shares or units paid out over a three- to five-year time frame based on achievement of financial or other performance goals. Restricted stock plans also became popular. These were outright grants of stock that vested over time as long as an executive stayed with the company.

It should be noted that stock options did not go away in the 1970s and early 1980s. But the way in which they were granted was very systematic, with a set amount given every year to top- and mid-level executives. The option grants had little to do with executive performance. Rather they were a perquisite of an executive's position and level within the company. They were an aspect of membership and executive privilege, not unlike the executive dining room and a corner office. Most executives saw their options not as a means to get rich quickly or amass great wealth but as a long-term means of building a personal nest egg over the course of their careers. In many ways the option plans of the 1970s and early 1980s resembled retirement and savings plans as opposed to motivationally driven incentive plans.

Economically the Jimmy Carter presidency is considered the worst period in the United States since the 1930s. One of the most important moves that Carter made may have cost him his presidency. Carter appointed Paul Volcker, a stalwart inflation-fighter, as chairman of the Federal Reserve. Volcker's monetary policy clamped down on credit, which made the economy worse in the short-term before it got better. But over time Volcker's policies whipped inflation and improved the health of the economy—and set the stage for the Reagan-era economic expansion of the 1980s. That could not have happened without a stable monetary policy.

The Reagan Administration introduced a huge stimulus package, with extraordinary tax cuts and other incentives, which made it easier for people to conduct business and do deals. The stock market began to grow and, lo and behold, stock options became popular again. By the end of the 1980s, companies were making such eye-popping grants of stock options and restricted stock that we had to come up with new terminology to describe them—hence the term, "mega grant." At that time "mega" referred to a grant equal to three times an executive's salary. Today, mega describes option grants of at least *eight times* the executive's salary *and bonus*. Among the notable cases of mega grants were Anthony O'Reilly of Heinz, Roberto Goizueta of Coca-Cola, and Michael Eisner of Disney. These executives received option and restricted stock grants worth an astronomical $80 million to $100 million—or more.

The focus in the 1980s and into the 1990s shifted strongly to stock performance, in part as an answer to shareholder concerns. Restricted stock became far less prevalent, as did other incentives that were considered to be giveaways to executives. In this environment options were seen as a preferred means to pay for performance because they had no value to executives unless the stock price went up. Executives only gained if shareholders gained. Since shareholder value was the rallying cry of the day, options were seen as a good way to align executive and shareholder interests.

More importantly the 1980s brought a fundamental revolution in how Corporate America viewed its own purpose, mission, and measures of success. There was a paradigm shift toward shareholder value and stock performance as the ultimate basis of how well or how poorly a corporation performed. Companies undertook major efforts to understand not just what made them profitable, but also what were the drivers of value—the buzzword of the day.

At this time we need to question the inordinate focus on share price and stock performance as the ultimate measure of corporate health and success. Clearly, in the past 10 years, we've taken that belief to the extreme by allowing our corporate executives to reap vast rewards based predominantly on the performance of their stock. As a consequence we've gotten away from rewarding executives and holding them accountable for managing the basic fundamentals of the businesses that they control. I question whether the principal job of management is to manage stock performance. It is the job of management to produce sustainable long-term profitable growth by producing and delivering valued products and services that meet a need in society.

LESSONS OF THE LBO

The 1980s also saw some major forces at work upsetting the status quo of corporations. Credit was freer than it had ever been. Investment banks were constantly finding new ways to borrow and lend money. Drexel Burnham and Michael Milken created the junk bond market, opening up public-debt financing to a whole new class of companies, borrowers and lenders. Kohlberg Kravis Roberts & Co. (KKR) and other firms led the investment groups that bought companies by borrowing against the company's assets in what became known as "leveraged buyouts," or LBOs. Usually, a small group of managers of the acquiring company also became partial owners as part of the transaction.

Groups of executives also organized company buyouts in which they borrowed as much money as they could. They sought the assistance of an investment bank to borrow the rest of the money required to buy the company from shareholders. These management buyouts or MBOs were very similar to LBOs in that the company's assets were pledged in order to borrow the funds required to pay shareholders for their stock.

After the LBO or MBO was completed, the company was "private," meaning that all of the shares previously owned by a large number of shareholders and traded on a stock exchange were now held by a small group of investors and were no longer publicly traded. Those investors typically included 10 to 20 of the company's executives who had mortgaged their homes and cashed in their personal savings to acquire significant stakes in the company. Now personally at risk, the same executives who had run these vast, slow-moving bureaucracies started making bold decisions to dramatically cut expenses and sell off major divisions.

Huge conglomerates like Beatrice Foods Company and the former Borg Warner Corp. that were built over decades were disassembled or pared down to their core in one to two years. Familiar corporate names disappeared overnight and thousands of people lost their jobs. Nonetheless, it showed that senior executives of many large corporations could—if properly motivated—think and act like entrepreneurs. The companies they owned and managed often became more streamlined, more competitive, and stronger for the future.

BorgWarner Inc., which had once been part of a huge holding company, provides a powerful example of the LBO experience. Today this lean and cost-conscious company is the best-performing major automotive supplier in the industry. Back in the 1970s, however, it was part of a conglomerate put together under the prevailing belief in economies of scale, which supposedly would allow a single management team to oversee and run diverse operations across several industries. Another classic example was Beatrice, which was also a conglomeration of businesses, many having little to do with each other. The idea in those days, however, was that if management could be successful in one business, why not in two, three, four, or more diverse areas?

By the early 1980s, however, it had become apparent that this strategy did not work. A single management structure was less effective in running operations across several industries than separate leadership teams. The individual parts were worth more than the whole.

In the case of the former Borg Warner Corp., it began shedding underperforming assets after the leveraged buyout in 1987. By 1993 two separate entities remained: Borg-Warner Automotive and Borg-Warner Securities. Each went public in separate transactions in 1993.

Borg-Warner Automotive eventually changed its name to Borg Warner Inc.

Working with BorgWarner over the past several years, it is apparent to me how this company has benefited hugely from having been an LBO. It is extremely cost-conscious and focused on cash flow and return on capital. Acutely aware of the capital it uses in the business, BorgWarner has one of the leanest corporate structures I have seen: this $3 billion company with six divisions is run by about 60 people who occupy only two floors of a building that had once been entirely occupied as the corporate headquarters of the old conglomerate. They are pared down to the core and only focus on what they do well.

One of the more unusual yet most impressive MBOs was the buyout and turnaround of Springfield ReManufacturing Corporation (SRC) in Springfield, Missouri. In the early 1980s SRC was a near bankrupt division of International Harvester. At the time SRC manager Jack Stack and 12 others from the company came up with $100,000 to put toward a loan of $9 million for a debt ratio of 89-to-1, which made it the most leveraged buyout in the United States at the time. More than just the amount of debt, what made SRC exceptional was its premise that everyone—from manager to hourly employee—wanted to win. Stack believed that workers are smart and can be educated in accounting and finance. With knowledge and information about the operations of the company—particularly the part of the company they manage or can influence—workers can take significant responsibility for the success of the company and foster continuous, positive change.

Stack's story, detailed in his book *The Great Game of Business*, chronicles the rise of SRC and what he sees as the essentials of the "equity game." Today, according to SRC's Web site (www. greatgame.com), the company has generated $54 million in equity value, with wealth that is widely distributed among people who helped create it. Shares of stock that were bought for 10 cents apiece are now worth more than $55.

As SRC and BorgWarner illustrate, MBOs and LBOs have a long and frequently successful history over the past 25 years. They rose in popularity in the 1980s as companies needed to restructure, reorganize, and refocus. Their lasting legacy, however, was the empowered owner/manager who worked hard to pay off debt and to increase shareholder value. Their motivation was simple: they owned significant stakes in the company and were personally at risk.

Traditional companies took note of these owner/managers who were making sweeping changes, taking risks, and putting plans into action. Granted since the MBO and LBO transactions had taken the companies private, these owner/managers often had more control of the companies, along with their investors. Still the large, publicly traded companies believed that with the right ownership stake they could motivate their top executives to make tough decisions and take bold actions.

LBOs and MBOs were interesting for another reason: they represented the second major wave of quick corporate takeovers in the last 40 years. The first major wave was in the 1960s when companies were bought and sold virtually overnight. If investor groups didn't like management, they could band together and take over the company as long as they had enough ownership and voting power. Curbing that practice the Williams Act of 1968 was passed. This act required investors buying more than 5 percent of a company's shares to file statements with the SEC to identify themselves, to state the source of their funding, and to declare their intentions. With this act the process of acquiring a company became so costly and time consuming for shareholder groups that the practice of quick takeovers virtually died.

Then in the 1980s, Milken's junk-bond financing revolution led to the second wave of takeovers, mainly through LBOs and MBOs. Investor groups staged takeovers and ousted the old management team in favor of a new team that usually included the investors. Corporate raiders, however, were labeled the bad guys, and states enacted legislation that effectively put up enough red tape to impede takeovers. But that wasn't the only thing impeded. The anti-takeover legislation curbed the "free market" for executive management.

Because of this, the ability of shareholders to threaten management with quick and decisive removal has been severely limited. Now shareholders have to go through a tremendously costly and time-consuming process to try to remove management. Keep in mind that the main reason company management is removed is when it is bad or performs poorly. But antitakeover legislation has removed shareholders' main weapon against poor management. By making takeovers more difficult, top executives have become almost untouchable. Even if they are terminated, almost all large public companies provide golden parachutes that give executives three times their salary and bonus, plus special option vesting and payouts and other benefits. There is virtually no financial downside.

The deeper problem, however, is that this reinforces a system in which there are many rewards and few consequences. The main tool companies have to motivate executives with is to provide more and more upside. Think about that for a moment. With my dog, a chocolate Labrador named Roosevelt, if I only had treats and no reprimands to train him, it would be a disaster. I'd have an ill-behaved dog weighing 400 pounds that I'd have to carry around in a wagon! Such is the state of executive compensation in America. For every system that provides rewards as an incentive for certain behaviors and actions, there must be consequences and disciplinary actions. For executives, the ultimate discipline is swift removal and without an expensive buyout.

WHEN EXECUTIVES BECOME OWNERS

The growing corporate rationale of the early 1990s was that executives could and should become "owners." But how could this be done without having to endure the pain and disruption of a leveraged buyout? The answer was simple and straightforward: executives would be required to own stock. When that happened executives would go from being loyal to the corporation to becoming loyal to the shareholder. Across Corporate America CEOs and other top executives were required to hold a specified multiple of their salary in stock. It was one of the fastest moving waves in governance at the time. By the mid-1990s more than half of the major publicly traded companies had requirements or guidelines that executives own stock. Companies typically required executives to own two to five times their annual salary in company stock. In the end many of these guidelines were not well enforced. One notable exception is the Xerox Corporation. The company withheld future option grants to executives who did not hold the required amount of stock. These exceptions were few and far between. Nonetheless, stock ownership mandates sure looked good on paper.

With the rise of executive stock ownership, corporate success was measured largely by stock price. Ironically it was the rapid rise of stock prices and the market in general that distracted the public eye from monitoring whether stock-ownership requirements were being met. The problem with stock ownership, from the executives' point of view, was that it took money out their pockets up front since they had to purchase the shares—and often a substantial amount of shares.

The answer looked like a panacea: the stock option. It had all the gain of stock ownership without any of the pain. Companies did not have to "pay" for the stock options granted to executives. Executives did not have to put up any money to receive them. The options gave the executives a financial interest that was similar but not the same as true ownership. Not surprisingly stock option grants became the fastest growing component in executive compensation packages. Many companies even allowed executives to count options as part of their stock ownership, which took the teeth out of the requirements.

Adding fuel to the fire of stock option grants was Section 162(m) of the Internal Revenue Code, part of the "antigreed legislation" passed in 1994. Section 162(m) capped an employer's annual deduction for the compensation of its top executives at $1 million in cash, unless certain criteria were met. Stock options, however, were exempt from the Section 162(m) salary cap, as long as they were part of a plan approved by shareholders. Since shareholders approved virtually all corporate stock option programs, large stock option grants proved to be an effective way to skirt Section 162(m) limitations and give large compensation packages to executives.

Stock options looked like financial manna from heaven in the 1990s so few people stopped to wonder what price was being paid for them. Yes they were free under current accounting. But they still carried a tremendous hidden cost to the company.

THE ROLE OF BOARDS IN COMPENSATION

The root of the executive compensation problem is an inherent lack of board independence and a corresponding lack of senior management accountability. As cited in Chapter 1, corporate directors are often a network of individuals, many of whom sit on each other's boards. The belief is that people who are successful in one industry bring valuable experience as board members to other, noncompeting companies. The fact that they belong to the same "class" as the CEO, i.e., corporate leaders with wealth and position, adds a sense of civility and camaraderie.

Don't get me wrong. In corporate boardrooms directors discuss and disagree as they hash out the issues before them. But rarely do directors want to deviate from the status quo. They rely very heavily on what "other companies" do. Far too often boards of directors maintain the accepted norm. In my experience consulting with company management and directors, seldom do I see board members challenging standard practices. In cordial and professional atmospheres they conduct the business at hand but in general avoid the tough and difficult questions. It's as if there is some implied agreement among board members: I won't make you look bad if you don't make me look bad. In the case of stock options, there has been a willingness among boards of directors to go along with what everyone else is doing. If other CEOs and other boards approved it, then it must be okay.

Clearly nowhere is the lack of board independence more apparent than in executive compensation. The Conference Board took on the topic with its Commission on Public Trust and Private Enterprise, which included representatives such as Intel CEO Andy Grove and former CSX CEO John Snow (now U.S. Treasury Secretary), former Fed Chairman Paul Volcker, and former SEC Chairman Arthur Levitt, Jr.

"The Commission shares the public's anger at the misconduct leading to the breakdown of public trust which grew out of the scandals at Enron, WorldCom, and other companies," the commission's report stated. [7]

"These egregious failures evidence a clear breach of the basic concept that underlies corporate capitalism—which is that investors entrust their assets to management while boards of directors over-see management so that the potential for conflict of interest between owners and managers is policed." the commission added.

Indeed the corporate scandals and public outrage over the apparent lack of board scrutiny of executive compensation under-mines the true spirit of capitalism. In order for capitalism to work, the system must include a clearly defined set of rewards linked to specific goals and targets. When wealth is accumulated only for its own sake rather than a reward for one's labor, ideas, investments, time, and talent, there is potential for abuse.

The Conference Board commission noted that there has been a "perfect storm" in executive compensation—"a confluence of events in the compensation area which created an environment ripe for abuse," which included lax behavior on the part of some boards of directors. The commission also noted a lack of independence on the part of compensation consultants, who have overly close rela-tionships with management.

Compensation consultants are partly to blame for this. We fed endless streams of data to corporate management and boards, showing them in excruciating and sophisticated analytical detail what other companies were doing. Part of the phenomenon was the way in which we presented the data: the practices of the median companies, the practices at the 75th percentile, and the practices at the 25th percentile. By definition half of the companies are always above the median and half are always below. When it comes to com-pensation, however, no one wants to set standards below the median—especially for their executives.

Under the tyranny of the median, the bottom half continually leapfrogs into the top half, only to raise the median bar again. This has been particularly true for stock options and long-term incen-tives, which experienced a meteoric rise from 1988 to 2001, growing by 400 to 600 percent (see Figure 2-1).

Compensation consultants are also partly to blame for pre-senting long-term incentive data only on an annual basis instead of showing the cumulative effect of several consecutive years of huge stock option grants. All these factors add up to what has become an untenable situation. Here's how The Conference Board's commis-

FIGURE 2-1

Rise in Executive Stock Options

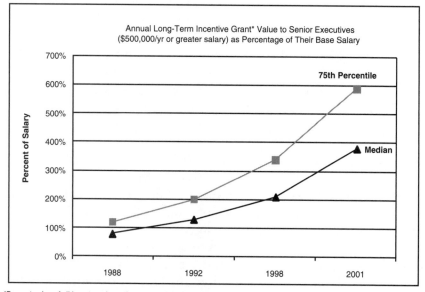

*Present value of all long-term incentives granted, including Black-Scholes value of stock options. Values are annualized to reflect how frequently the long-term incentives are granted.

Source: The Delves Group Compensation Library

sion describes the current state of executive compensation and corporate governance:

- "Excessive use of stock options—particularly fixed price options—was encouraged by the fact that fixed price options do not result in a charge to earnings, while they provide the added benefit of substantial tax deductions;

- "The speculative nature of stock options led, in some cases, to their being undervalued by executives to whom they were granted, which in turn necessitated higher levels of grants;

- "Board of directors became lax in performing their historical duty to monitor compensation;

- "The balance in the relationship between the board, management and compensation consultants, has, in too many cases, been skewed to produce an overly close relationship between consultants and management;
- "The use of stock options and other equity-based incentives resulted in an enormous incentive to manage companies for short-term stock price gains;
- "The unprecedented bull market led to massive, unanticipated gains from options unrelated to management's operating performance."

Not only were the conditions ripe for potential abuses of stock options, but also a lack of accounting for them encouraged their overuse. Without accounting for them, it became difficult for boards to measure their impact on the company. What is not measured, after all, is generally not well managed.

Without an adequate system to account for and measure the cost of stock options, boards of directors did not effectively manage the magnitude of what was granted. Instead of questioning what the corporation and its shareholders were getting in return for such lucrative compensation packages, boards continued to approve ever increasing grants for top executives. Once again because stock options were free according to the old accounting, it seemed like the perfect incentive, based on the theory that stock ownership in any form would align executives' interests with those of shareholders.

STOCK OPTIONS FOR START-UPS AND THE TECHNOLOGY REVOLUTION

Stock options had the ability to bestow "ownership" on executives who could earn a piece of the corporation through their toil. In concept this sounds noble and appeals to our American capitalistic natures. Just like the homesteaders who worked the soil and in time owned the land, the corporate pioneers could earn their ownership. Nowhere was this practice more prevalent than in the technology companies and dot-coms of the 1990s.

In these startups *everybody* received stock options—from CEO to entry-level employee. With options they shared the wealth, or more accurately, the promise of wealth. According to a study by the National Center for Employee Ownership (NCEO), from 1992 to 1997 biotechnology and computer companies granted 55 percent of their stock options to nonmanagement employees. Interestingly the study—reflecting the strong economic conditions of the 1990s—drew a close parallel between the rise in stock option grants, the tightening of the labor market, and high-technology job creation.

The spread of stock options grants also had the effect of transferring a growing portion of the future value of the company from the hands of shareholders into the hands of employees and managers. As Figure 2-2 illustrates, the percentage of outstanding stock devoted to stock option plans increased dramatically, rising from 3 to 5 percent in 1990 to 12 to 15 percent among general industry companies in 2001. In high-technology companies the average is much higher—18 to 25 percent, with some companies as high as 30 to 40 percent.

The proliferation of stock options through the employee ranks is not just confined to technology start-ups. Large-cap technology

FIGURE 2-2

The Percentage of Outstanding Stock Devoted to Stock Options*

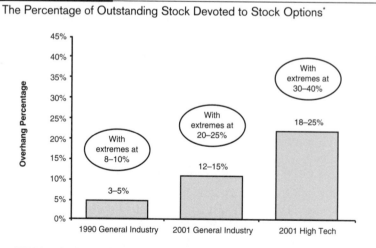

*2002 Investor Responsibility Research Center
Note: Percentages reflect total options granted plus total shares reserved for future option grants, divided by the total number of shares outstanding.

companies such as Microsoft, Cisco Systems, and Intel have been very liberal in their granting of stock options to virtually all employees. When Intel was founded in 1968, options were granted to the professional staff, which represented about one-third of the workforce, the *Wall Street Journal* reported. In the mid-1990s Intel opted to make stock options available to all full-time employees. "Like many other technology companies, the chip maker has used options heavily as a recruiting and retention tool. Grants can range up to 200,000 options," the *Journal* reported.[8]

Needless to say with such broad-based options, Intel opposes expensing them and continues to lobby against such proposals. In 2001 Intel estimated that expensing options would have reduced its earnings from $1.3 billion to $254 million.

A SKEWED INCENTIVE SYSTEM

While it's hard to fault the "share the wealth" philosophy behind the broad-based options plans, a problem occurs when these potentially lucrative incentives taint the corporate culture. There are dozens of stories and anecdotes out of the hi-tech world of millionaires, paper millionaires, and would-be paper millionaires amassing their fortunes from stock options. In the height of the technology boom, legions of 20-somethings went to work for technology firms, Internet boutiques, and dot-com start-ups for the promise of wealth when the company "went public" in the not-too-distant future. They signed up to work tirelessly for three or four years, sometimes for low pay, for these seemingly magical options that in a few years' time would turn into small fortunes. Retire at 30? Live on a beach with plenty of "f-you money" in the bank? All of it seemed to be within the realm of possibility in the world of technology and stock options.

This highly skewed incentive system, however, strikes at the heart of capitalism, which certainly condones the reaping of rewards for one's labor but not the pursuit of an idle life of leisure at age 29. The technology phenomenon brought with it the mantra of "work hard, get rich quick, and leave." But that was just the kind of mindset that was embraced by these counterculture firms, where blue jeans and cutoff shorts were part of the corporate uniform and entrepreneurial spirit meant "we don't need no stinking bosses."

The corporate culture was reflected in things like cool lunchrooms and hip cubicles. I've been in a hundred of those places and with the popping of the technology bubble in 2000 and into 2001, most of them aren't there anymore.

During their heyday they were able to attract 20-somethings and even some 30- and 40-somethings who thought this was really "it" for them. With a fist full of stock options, they knew what was in store for them: wealth and freedom. All they had to do was work their tails off in the meantime. As tempting as this was, it was not a healthy reason to go to work for a company. The real reasons to go to work for a company are because you fit in with the corporate culture, the job makes sense for your career path, you love the products, believe in the mission of the company, and like the people you work with—not solely because you want to get rich in a hurry.

The pendulum of ethical behavior is now swinging back to equilibrium. The bursting of the Nasdaq bubble and the decline of the overall stock market has left many stock options underwater—meaning the current market price of the stock is far below the exercise price of the options. The value of these options is far less than when they were first granted—and well below what employees had hoped it would be. This is a sobering reality for many technology executives and employees alike; they are now faced with the reality of paper fortunes that aren't worth much more than the paper itself.

This is the taste of bitter medicine that is necessary to correct the current problem of executive compensation and to ensure a healthy corporate environment going forward. Reining in excessive stock option grants, balancing pay with performance, and measuring the total cost of compensation are steps that must be undertaken by companies and their boards of directors. This is not to curb the spirit of capitalism. Rather the pursuit of wealth should carry with it its own code of ethical behavior including effective systems of accountability.

CHAPTER THREE

The Accounting Story

Expensing employee stock options is hardly a new concept. Over the years there has been much discussion about how to account for these financial instruments. Until recently, however, Corporate America has kept up a united front in opposition to expensing options. Now the accounting rules are about to change, requiring companies to account for options as expenses on their income statements instead of only listing them as footnotes. While this is significant progress, focusing only on the accounting rules belies the full extent of the story.

Accounting for options is a saga with its share of intrigue and compromise behind the scenes, all of which seems fitting for such high-risk and largely misunderstood instruments. The accounting rules, while a step in the right direction, are not the complete solution to what will remain a difficult and emotionally charged problem. These rules alone will not assure us that companies will assume full accountability and risk management where options are concerned. To do that companies will have to ask themselves what few have even pondered yet: what is the true economic cost of options?

To answer that question, let's examine how far we have come on the expensing of options. The issue of accounting for options was first raised in the early 1950s. But with no effective means to value options at that time, the discussions on accounting for them did not go very far. Then, in 1972, the Accounting Principles Board (APB)—the predecessor to the Financial Accounting Standards Board (FASB)—issued its Opinion Number 25 (APB 25). Under APB 25 options were treated as essentially "free," meaning they did not have to be expensed on a company's income statement as long as they met certain criteria, such as having a fixed exercise price and a fixed number of shares.

Interestingly, in 1973, Myron Scholes, who would later win the Nobel Prize in economics for his work, and Fischer Black jointly published the Black-Scholes model for valuing options. While the model is widely known as Black-Scholes, Robert Merton also was instrumental in its development and shared the Nobel Prize for it with Scholes after Black's death. Before Black-Scholes there was no readily available methodology for valuing options. Today Black-Scholes and its variants are the most widely used valuation models.

The publication of Black-Scholes in 1973 also coincided with the founding of the Chicago Board Options Exchange (CBOE), which today is the world's largest options exchange. Before 1973 options were traded on an unregulated basis. Of course options granted as part of compensation and incentive packages are not tradable. Still the founding of a fair and orderly marketplace for options underscored what was then a new concept: options had an understood and quantifiable value.

Over the next two decades stock options grew in popularity and usage as part of compensation packages. As a result the FASB began a campaign in the 1980s requiring them to be expensed. Moving into the 1990s the FASB became more earnest in its quest. When it attempted to make this expense ruling in 1993 and 1994, however, the board was nearly pummeled out of existence by CEO groups, institutional investors, the major accounting firms, the Securities and Exchange Commission (SEC), Congress, and the White House. As the FASB itself explained: "When the FASB developed FAS 123 (Financing Accounting Standard 123) in the mid-1990s, the Board proposed requiring that [expensing] treatment because it believed that this was the best way to report the effect of employee stock options in a company's financial statements. The FASB modified that proposal in the face of strong opposition by many in the business community and in Congress that directly threatened the existence of the FASB as an independent standard setter."[9]

The debate over the expensing of stock options also embroiled the major accounting firms, which at first had supported the FASB requirement but then withdrew it as corporate opposition to the expense mounted. Curiously, the same thing occurred in Congress, which at first requested the FASB to take on this issue and later undermined the accounting board when CEO and corporate lobbying intensified. What happened behind the scenes of that debate reveals much about the controversial nature of options accounting. It also adds to the still unfolding tale of the accounting profession and more specifically to the thorny question of where auditing practices leave off and client consulting begins.

Like much in accounting these days, this story is viewed in retrospect through the lens of the Enron scandal and the downfall of its auditor Arthur Andersen. As this story unfolds, the reality of the debate surrounding the FASB's attempts to require the expensing of options is exposed. Corporate America was on the brink of an important decision, and it is eye-opening to see what led to the final result—and how that decision came about. In the end it tells a sad tale that strikes at the heart and soul of corporate accountability.

BEHIND THE SCENES OF THE ACCOUNTING DEBATE

The FASB's efforts in the early 1990s to require the expensing of options were fueled in part by the investor outrage at the time over excessive executive pay. The board had long believed that option grants should be expensed, and with shareholder interests seemingly on its side, the accounting board felt the time was right to make the necessary rule changes.

When the FASB reached its initial conclusions about expensing options, it sought comment on its proposed rule, including from the accounting profession. At first the board received the backing of the major accounting firms, including Arthur Andersen's standards-setting group the Accounting Principles Group. Andersen's group went so far as to prepare position papers in favor of the rule. This position, however, would not be held for long.

Larry Weinbach, Andersen's CEO at the time, and other senior managers of the firm disagreed with the Accounting Principles Group, saying that the firm could not support the position of the

FASB. The reason? Strong opposition by clients, in particular high-technology firms.

In a four-part series on the fall of Andersen, *Crain's Chicago Business* quoted Arthur Wyatt, a member and former chairman of Andersen's standards-setting body, on the change of heart regarding option expensing. Wyatt, who was nearing retirement in late 1992, recalled, "one of the guys came in and said we had to change our view on it. The rationale given was we had too many clients unhappy with the previous position we had taken (in favor of option expensing)."[10]

Apparently this had never happened before in the firm's history. Up until this point Andersen's policy was that the Accounting Principles Group was above the rest of the firm and could not be tainted or tempted by the lobbying of clients. In fact Andersen had been a leader in creating and maintaining high standards in the accounting profession.

But times had clearly changed at Andersen as it went from an auditing company to a consulting firm as well. Technology companies had granted huge numbers of options and were therefore vehemently opposed to the proposed FASB rule. Tech firms were also a growing constituency among Andersen's clients. When they let their opposition to the accounting rule be known, Andersen bowed to the pressure.

Sadder still was the apparent *quid pro quo* in Andersen's sudden shift of position. In exchange for a change of position on the FASB rule tech companies had apparently pledged to lobby Congress for tort reform for the accounting profession. This reform would limit the liability of individual partners in cases of inaccurate audits and other actions for which the firm was found liable. The standing regulation at the time required the accounting firms that audited public companies to be general partnerships in which each partner was individually, jointly, and severally liable for all actions of the firm. When tort reform passed, however, the individual liability of partners was greatly reduced.

Both sides got what they wanted. Technology firms were not required to expense options, and accounting firm partners had limited liability on firm actions. Did that open the door for the type of behavior that led to Enron's high-risk actions and questionable accounting, which received the apparent blessing of its auditor? The evidence certainly points in that direction.

While it does not detail the technology firms' role in supporting tort reform for accounting firms, the *Crain's* article does corroborate the growing influence of Andersen's technology clients. Referring to the ill-fated end of the options expensing debate, the article states, "FASB and the Securities and Exchange Commission (SEC) acquiesced in the wake of the 1994 mid-term elections, which put both houses of Congress under Republican control for the first time in 40 years and strengthened the lobbying power of the accounting industry. The apparent victory would hold profound implications for Andersen. It symbolized the grip that technology clients had gained on the firm, not as an auditor but as a consultant, reaping head-spinning fees."[10]

Interestingly, the only recorded vote in Congress on stock options took place in 1994, when the Senate approved by a vote of 88 to 9 a nonbinding resolution proposed by Sen. Joseph Lieberman (D-Conn) urging the FASB not to go forward with its proposal to expense options. This vote followed an intense lobbying campaign, including a one-day event in March 1994 in which 100 CEOs flew to Washington to lobby personally members of Congress against expensing options. While supporters of stock option expensing, led by Sen. Carl Levin (D-Mich), managed to add a provision to the resolution declaring that Congress ought to respect the independence of the FASB and not politicize accounting rules, the Senate vote was seen as sending a political warning to the FASB.

When the FASB, bruised and battle scarred, finally did adopt FAS 123, it had backed off from requiring that options be expensed. While the board maintained its position that options *should* be expensed, FAS 123 said that options *could* be expensed. If they weren't expensed (and the vast majority of companies did not opt to expense them), then they had to be disclosed in footnotes to the company's financial statements.

The FASB's own statement about FAS 123 has a note of what, at least in hindsight, sounds like defeat: "The board chose a disclosure-based solution for stock-based employee compensation to bring closure to the divisive debate on this issue—not because it believes that solution is the best way to improve financial accounting and reporting."[9]

FASB'S RENEWED CAMPAIGN

The FASB may have lost that battle but it appears to be winning the war. In its renewed campaign to require option expensing, the FASB gained an important ally: Federal Reserve Board Chairman Alan Greenspan. In an address before the 2002 Financial Markets Conference of the Federal Reserve Bank of Atlanta delivered in May of that year, Greenspan championed option expensing as potentially bolstering investor confidence and helping the economy as a whole.

"The seemingly narrow accounting matter of option expensing is, in fact, critically important for the accurate representation of corporate performance," Greenspan said in his remarks. "And accurate reporting, in turn, is central to the functioning of free-market capitalism—the system that has brought such a high level of prosperity to our country."

Just as in the early 1990s, when investors were outraged over excessive executive compensation, the FASB is once again emboldened to take action on this controversial issue. Many investors and much of the public at large have taken a decidedly anticorporate stance, looking for someone to blame for everything from the drop in stock prices to the weakness in the economy. In a world of corporate reform, the option expense is some of the low-hanging fruit.

In a Motley Fool column (www.fool.com), Bill Mann accurately portrayed how many savvy investors felt over options and the reluctance of some firms—particularly technology—to expense them. "Companies are afraid that if they have to show the true economic cost of options, earnings will be lower, and their share prices will drop. Big deal! If stock options provide a distorted picture of performance to the end shareholder, then we're not talking about making financial statements look worse. We're talking about making them look accurate."[11]

With the Enron/Andersen saga filling the news headlines and the concerns over potential accounting scandals taking a toll on share prices, companies needed to take decisive action to improve investor confidence. Enter Coca-Cola. In July 2002 the soft drink company suddenly announced it would deduct stock options from its earnings. Until that time, aircraft manufacturer Boeing and retailer Winn-Dixie Stores were the only major corporations that expensed options. Every other firm merely made note of the amount of stock options granted in financial footnotes, as allowed under the existing accounting rules.

Soon after Coca-Cola made its announcement, Bank One, The Washington Post Company, and Amazon.com said they too would begin expensing options. By the end of 2002 more than 100 companies had committed to expensing options. As billionaire investor and option expensing watchdog Warren Buffett observed, "the time has come" for the reform of stock options.

As one would expect the FASB was quick to praise the corporations that volunteered to expense. "The FASB applauds those companies because recognizing compensation expense relating to the fair value of employee stock options granted is the preferable approach under current U.S. accounting standards. . . . It is also the treatment advocated by an increasing number of investors and other users of financial statements," the FASB said in a statement issued July 31, 2002. "Until now, only a handful of companies elected to follow the preferable method."

The decision to expense options is more than just lip service on the part of companies. The action will impact earnings. In the case of Coca-Cola, the *Financial Times* reported that if the company had expensed options in 2001, it would have reduced net income from $3.97 billion to $3.77 billion and its earnings per share from $1.60 to $1.51.

A Bear Stearns study, as shown in Figure 3-1, found that the average company in the S&P 500 would have seen its earnings shrink by 8 percent in 2000 and by 20 percent in 2001 if options were factored in. At technology companies the expensing reduction would have been even greater due to larger grants to executives and broad-based plans that granted options to most employees. Executives at technology companies typically receive option grants that are 100 percent to 200 percent greater than grants given to their counterparts in nontech companies.

F I G U R E   3-1

Bear Stearns "Employee Stock Option Expense Report"—July 2002[*]

| | Option Expense as a Percentage of Earnings | | |
Industry	Expense as a percentage of earnings 1999	Expense as a percentage of earnings 2000	Expense as a percentage of earnings 2001
Advertising	260%	12%	11%
Application Software	221%	71%	55%
Computer Hardware	49%	17%	10%
Semiconductor Hardware	42%	11%	21%
Health Care Distributors & Services	35%	18%	26%
Health Care Supplies	30%	16%	11%
Biotechnology	28%	20%	12%
Employment Services	25%	12%	10%
Diversified Commercial Services	24%	16%	29%
Aluminum	20%	11%	10%
Environmental Services	17%	219%	N/M
Health Care Equipment	17%	10%	11%
Specialty Store	15%	12%	10%
Oil & Gas Equipment & Services	14%	16%	29%
Construction & Engineering	12%	11%	33%
Electronic Equipment & Instruments	N/M	27%	15%
Gold	N/M	N/M	44%
Internet Software & Services	N/M	1887%	664%
Movies and Entertainment	N/M	58%	25%
Networking Equipment	N/M	53%	27%
Semiconductors	N/M	14%	14%
Telecommunications Equipment	N/M	150%	31%

N/M—Percentage decline is not meaningful since the group has reported a loss.
[*]Bear Stearns Accounting Issues, *Employees Stock Option Expense, Is the Time Right for a Change?*, July 2002. Used by permission.

According to *Fortune Magazine*, the effect of expensing options would result in a 59 percent reduction in Dell Computer's earnings, a 79 percent reduction for Intel, and a 171 percent reduction for Cisco Systems Inc. for the year 2001.[12]

Little wonder, then, that technology firms have been so outspoken in their opposition to option expensing. The American Electronics Association (AeA), which claims some 3500 member-companies in the high-tech industry, praised the defeat of a senate amendment sponsored by Republican Senator John McCain of Arizona requiring the expensing of stock options. In a statement, the AeA said, "The high-tech industry would be disproportionately affected by changes to accounting rules regarding the expensing of stock options." Of course they would be disproportionately affected. Technology firms have used options in far greater quantities than other firms. This is still no reason to maintain bad accounting.

Despite continued opposition by technology firms, option expensing is nearly a *fait accompli*. Throughout 2003 the FASB has been seeking commentary on its proposed rules, which will likely take effect the following year. The centerpiece of the new accounting rules will be the terms and conditions of option expensing and the method of valuing options. The FASB and its London-based counterpart, the International Accounting Standards Board (IASB), have indicated that their rules will reflect the fair value of options as of the grant date. But what does this mean?

MEASURING THE VALUE OF OPTIONS

In determining the accounting expense for options, there are two main questions: what is the measurement date and what is the valuation method?

Addressing the first question there are three possible measurement dates: the date options are granted, the date they vest or become exercisable, and the date they are actually exercised. There are two principal methods of determining value. One method is the intrinsic value, which is the spread between the exercise price of the option and the market price of the stock. The second is the fair value method, which is the market value of the stock option instrument itself.

It is the combination of these two key variables that determines how much the expense will be and when it will be incurred. Let's take them one at a time.

First consider the measurement date. Current accounting rules under APB 25 require that the measurement date be the date when you first know the exercise price and the number of shares under the option. In a traditional option both of these factors are known at the grant date. Therefore the grant date is used as the measurement date. However if either the number of shares or the exercise price can change or is variable, then the measurement date is postponed until these are known. The implications of this will be discussed later in this chapter.

To adopt fully the expensing of options under FAS 123, it is required that the measurement date be the grant date. The grant date is also the measurement date under the proposed new accounting rules.

The other factor to consider is the valuation method. Under APB 25 the valuation method is the intrinsic value, the spread between market price and exercise price. (Under FAS 123 and the proposed new rules, the valuation method is the fair value.) Under APB 25 if you know the exercise price and the number of shares under the option at the time it is granted—and you usually do—then the measurement date is the grant date. Since the valuation method under APB 25 is intrinsic value, the expense will reflect the intrinsic value as of the grant date. If the option exercise price is equal to the market price of the stock as of the grant date—which is the case in virtually all option grants—then the intrinsic value as of the grant date is zero.

To show how expensing works under APB 25, let's take the hypothetical example of a company that grants an executive on January 1, 2003, an option to purchase 1000 shares of stock for $25 per share. (We'll also assume that the options vest—become exercisable—after three years, and do not expire for 10 years.) The market price of the stock at the time is also $25. Under APB 25 since the number of shares and the exercise price are known, the measurement date is the grant date. The intrinsic value is the difference between the $25 exercise price and the $25 share price. Thus the intrinsic value is zero, and the expense for these options is zero.

However, under APB 25, if either the exercise price or the number of shares is unknown or variable, then the measurement date is postponed until both these facts are known. For example, if the options were to vest based on performance (and there is a possibility that some of the options might not vest), then the number of shares could not be determined until the vesting performance requirements are met. The measurement date is then postponed until that time.

Let's assume that the option for 1000 shares vested at the end of three years, based upon the company's financial performance over that time period. The executive could earn the right to exercise the full 1000 shares or the right to exercise some portion of those shares, depending upon how the company performed. Thus the number of shares could not be determined until the end of the three-year performance period. In this case the end of the three-year period becomes the measurement date. The intrinsic value could not be fixed until the measurement date. Until that time it is variable.

If at the end of the three-year period the stock price is $40, then the intrinsic value would be $15 ($40 minus the $25 exercise price) and the expense would be $15 per share for every share that has vested. In the meantime, however, the potential expense would have to be estimated and amortized over the three-year performance vesting period. This is another complicating factor. As Figure 3-2 shows, each quarter the company would have to determine the spread between the exercise price and the market price and adjust its quarterly expense—up or down—accordingly.

The variable accounting expense is unpredictable and potentially large. These are two things that company accountants and CFOs hate; they want to avoid these kinds of expenses at all cost. This explains why 99 percent of stock options have a fixed price and a fixed grant date and an exercise price equal to the market price of the stock as of the grant date. Under APB 25 this yields zero expense.

This strange juxtaposition of arcane accounting requirements—which must be met to achieve the zero expense—has led to the proliferation of these plain vanilla stock option grants with no performance strings attached. The reason is virtually any performance requirement would result in variable accounting. For at least the last 30 years, the accounting "tail" has wagged the "big dog" of executive compensation.

FIGURE 3-2

Performace-Based Variable Accounting

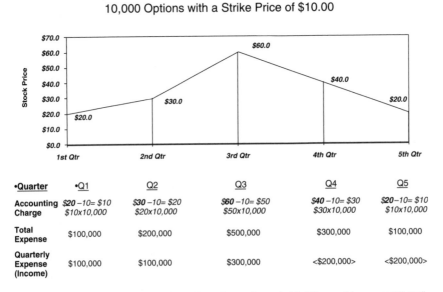

10,000 Options with a Strike Price of $10.00

•Quarter	•Q1	Q2	Q3	Q4	Q5
Accounting Charge	$20 –10= $10 $10x10,000	$30 –10= $20 $20x10,000	$60 –10= $50 $50x10,000	$40 –10= $30 $30x10,000	$20 –10= $10 $10x10,000
Total Expense	$100,000	$200,000	$500,000	$300,000	$100,000
Quarterly Expense (Income)	$100,000	$100,000	$300,000	<$200,000>	<$200,000>

Note: The variable expense is amortized over the option vesting period. In this case it is assumed that all of the options are vested.

DETERMINING FAIR VALUE

The reign of APB 25 and zero expense accounting is coming to an end. Under the recommended but not required rules of the existing FAS 123 and, more importantly, under the proposed new rules, the measurement date for options is still the grant date. The valuation method changes, however, from intrinsic value to fair value. Therein lies the big debate: how do you determine the fair value?

The preferred method of determining fair value has been the Black-Scholes option pricing model, which typically results in a fair value estimate of 30 percent to 50 percent of the face value of the option. For example, the 1000-share option grant with a market exercise price of $25 would have a face value of $25,000, and an estimated fair value using Black-Scholes of $7500 to $12,500. This value would be the total expense for these options, determined at the grant date and amortized over the option vesting period. Thus, if the expense were $12,500 and the options vested at the end of three years, the annual expense for each of those years would be approximately $4167.

If, under the new rules, the options have performance features—such as vesting based upon performance or an accelerating exercise price—they will still have a fixed expense as of the grant date (unlike APB 25, which would have required a variable expense). This allows far more flexibility in designing performance-based options and other incentives without being penalized with adverse accounting.

Given all these factors, the FASB/IASB approach seems to make the most sense from an accounting perspective. The fair value treatment recognizes that the options are not "free" at the time they are granted but have some determinable value. Using the grant date gives companies a set point in time at which to fix the expense.

As an aside, it should be noted that for tax purposes the Internal Revenue Service has always used and will continue to use the intrinsic value at exercise date. For example, if an option has an exercise price of $10 and the stock is trading at $100, the individual who exercises that option buys a $100 stock for $10. That results in $90-per-share in taxable income for the individual and a $90-per-share expense (or tax deduction) for the company. There has never been any argument against this treatment, perhaps because companies get a valuable tax deduction from it.

Under the current and proposed accounting rules, the fair value approach will require some valuation model to be used. I believe that option pricing models like Black-Scholes and more recently developed variants are an effective way to determine the expense, as long as we make appropriate adjustments for terminations, forfeitures, and early exercise.

Black-Scholes and its variants are already widely used to communicate to employees and executives as well as to the shareholders and investors the value of their option packages. John Biggs, then chairman and CEO of pension fund TIAA-CREF, noted in his testimony before the Senate Committee on Banking, Housing and Urban Affairs, "I can assure [you] that high-tech executives in Silicon Valley use Black-Scholes to communicate total compensation to employees. Those same executives know that having to show the results of that calculation to shareholders would reduce or even eliminate the earnings of their companies."[13]

It should come as no surprise that many corporate managers and executives are now complaining that the Black-Scholes option pricing model overstates the value of their stock options. Yet how can you argue with a pricing methodology that has been used to value millions of option transactions every day for the past 30 years? The reluctance to accept Black-Scholes tells us that corporate executives and employees undervalue options; they do not recognize what options are truly worth. The market value of options is significantly more, as Black-Scholes indicates, than most executives and employees are willing to admit. This is understandable since stock options are highly risky derivative securities that few individual investors would have in their portfolios in any significant numbers. Option pricing models estimate the cost of options to the company, which is almost always greater than the value of the options to the executive receiving them.

Just as most stocks are worth more as part of a diversified investment portfolio so are the stocks or options that are granted as incentives. When granted in vast numbers, options are part of a highly undiversified portfolio. Because of their high-risk characteristics and the fact that they cannot be sold or traded, options are not fully valued by the employees who receive them. The companies complaining about the valuation methodology are like the lead-foot drivers who try to blame their speedometers when they're ticketed for speeding. In both instances the problem is not with the methodology or measurement; the problem is in the "driver's seat." When it comes to executive compensation, options have been doing the driving for far too long. The disparity between the Black-Scholes value and the value perceived by executives and employees delivers a strong message.

The perceived lack of worth of options by executives and employees shows that valuable shareholder resources have been misused in the granting of these options. These resources could have been spent more effectively on other incentive vehicles to the benefit of the company, its shareholders, and its employees.

Looking at this issue more broadly, the misuse of resources should come as no surprise. Any time that we neglect to accurately account for or measure the cost of what we are spending on something—especially something we like—most people will overspend. This is exactly what corporations have done. By failing to accurately account for and value options, they have overspent corporate resources for them.

This is compounded by the fact that the accounting rule makers at the FASB and IASB have not considered the true economic cost of stock options. The proposed accounting rules that have been set forth by the FASB and IASB are a pragmatic and sensible compromise. While accountants would like to make this a simple matter—with a simple and easily determined expense—the true economic cost is a far more complex issue that must be addressed by companies and their boards.

An option is a significant liability to the company. The problem, however, is that its true value is highly variable and hard to estimate. The potential economic cost could be very large or very small. In some cases that cost may be zero, which is why start-ups and companies with poor-performing stocks object to a fair value expense determined at the grant date.

On the other hand the true economic cost could greatly exceed the grant date expense. Using an example of an option with a $10 exercise price, the Black-Scholes option pricing model would generate a value and expense as of the grant date of $3 to $5 per share. However, if the stock price goes to $20 a share, then the potential economic cost to the company is the spread between the market price and the exercise price, or $10. If the stock goes to $50, the economic cost is $40. However, if the stock price fell to $5 a share, the economic cost would be zero.

The answer is not to avoid estimating the cost just because it's difficult. Human beings, after all, have tackled far more difficult things—from moon landings to decoding DNA—than determining the economic costs associated with stock options. Companies and their boards must recognize that the accounting issue is truly only the tip of the iceberg. The bulk of that iceberg lurking beneath the surface involves much more profound and high-impact issues concerning executive compensation and board governance. They must be accountable to their shareholders for wisely deploying their resources to generate appropriate, measurable returns for the company.

A NEW CHAPTER IN THE STORY

Now you know the story. But it doesn't end there. It's time to add a
new chapter to the accounting story. To get that started, I spoke with
Jim Leisenring, board member of the International Accounting
Standards Board (IASB).

Leisenring may be the most outspoken advocate of stock option
expensing and has been for more than 10 years. In his mind, not only
does stock option expensing make sense, it is imperative for sound
accounting practices and fair executive compensation. In the early
1990s when the Financial Accounting Standards Board (FASB) tried
to adopt expensing, Leisenring (then a member of the FASB) was
among those who testified in favor of the plan before Congress.
Although the FASB failed at that time, in the face of mounting opposition from corporations, accounting firms, Congress, and the Securities and Exchange Commission (SEC), Leisenring sees a different
climate today. Leisenring predicts that the FASB will adopt an option
expensing rule, in part due to the support of the IASB.

Delves: Why are you so passionate about the stock option expensing
issue?

Leisenring: Actually I'm not any more passionate about this particular
issue than I am other issues. I feel just as strongly about proper accounting for derivatives and other items that are not properly accounted for.
To me not having a mandatory expense for options is just another issue
of bad accounting. I may appear more passionate about it because I
become apoplectic about the vacuous arguments against it—in particular when they're made by people who ought to know better.

I also think that, from a corporate management standpoint,
accounting shouldn't stand in the way of good compensation plans.
We ought to let management do whatever they do, and then judge
them on whether they did it badly or well based on the performance
of the company. I don't care if they pay everybody one million
options! The marketplace will judge whether this is good or bad.
Right now the way the accounting is, it causes people to use the types
of compensation systems that strike me as suboptimal. That's the
worst kind of an accounting standard.

Delves: It's an accounting standard that forces you in the wrong direction.

Leisenring: Or it forces you to make a bad choice. If I was running a big company and granting stock options, I would want the grant of options to be more focused. I would want performance incentives that would hopefully cause you to do your job better, specific to your primary responsibility.

Delves: But under the current ("old") accounting rules, FAS 123, you can't do that without variable accounting.

Leisenring: Exactly.

Delves: Do you think that the FASB is going to be able to enact new accounting rules this time, which will require option expensing?

Leisenring: Yes. For one thing, there is too much pressure. Too much international pressure from the IASB and pressure domestically. We keep saying that we have the superior accounting standards in the United States, so it will be harder for the FASB not to adopt it, if the IASB goes ahead. Also, more and more companies have been deciding to expense options. General Motors and a hundred others. It's not unanimous opposition any more.

Delves: When option expensing is mandated, at some companies the pay of the top five or ten people is going to be so huge it's going to be a line item on the income statement.

Leisenring: Yes. I think it's an issue of scrutiny. Too many compensation committees work off the basis of, what percentage of our shares are out there in options, and how many options does our CEO have versus somebody else's CEO. As if that was relevant!

Delves: Now that it appears that the FASB and the IASB will be requiring option expensing, let's take a look back in history to see how we got to the place we are today.

Leisenring: In the mid-1980s the FASB started working on stock options. But they couldn't resolve stock option accounting without first thinking more about what is a liability versus what is an equity instrument. They concluded that a stock option shouldn't be a liability but an equity instrument. That allowed them to resolve the measurement date issue as we don't typically re-measure equity instruments as we do liabilities.

Delves: And that measurement date was going to be either the grant date or would it be some other date?

Leisenring: I argued vociferously that the option didn't exist until the vesting date. I argued that an option by definition gave someone a right, and they didn't have that right until they got through the vesting process. I wanted vesting date, as did some others. But the majority of the board was in favor of grant date.

Since the definition between liability and equity has been changed somewhat at least in application since that debate, I can't legitimately argue that the contract, which grants the options, isn't, in itself, an equity instrument. It doesn't result in options yet, but promises to grant them. Most people concede that . . . And it is at vesting date that the option exists. But the contract to grant the options seems, in and of itself, to meet the definition of an equity instrument. Of course there are many more measurement problems at the grant date: are they or aren't they going to vest? They are not transferable. They are not exercisable through the vesting period. All of these issues must be considered and vesting date would be easier.

Delves: Once FASB decided to go with the grant date, that's when the debate really heated up.

Leisenring: After we got through the measurement date issue, that's when all the lobbying began. They argued, by and large, that you can't do this. You can't require expensing. It's too damaging. It will hurt the wrong people. I remember at the hearings one of the senators asked, "How do you respond to the people who will say there will be companies that will be deprived of capital or charged more for capital as a result of expensing?" I said, "What would you have accounting do? Not differentiate between companies? What you're saying is that we should make the company that grants no options look like the company that grants a million options. I don't think we should do that, any more than we should make the company that doesn't have a pension plan look like one that does have a pension plan." If people believe in market places, then they should advocate information that is neutral and evenhanded, and allow the capital markets to make their decisions based on that information.

Delves: In the end, of course, the FASB backed down from requiring option expensing. Instead FAS 123 was a compromise allowing companies to basically list options in a footnote. There was just too much opposition to the FASB plans to require expensing.

Leisenring: We had no support from Congress. The Senate was 88 to 9 against us. The SEC said to us, you're on your own. A lot of board members were upset that this sort of interference was going on and they said, we could spend a great deal of time and resources and still not improve accounting. I believe we had the ability to do something that was so obviously right, that we should have spent our effort in political battle. I think we could have made some great arguments in front of Congress that would have been persuasive and really addressed the executive greed issue. The Congressmen believed the options were for everybody ... But as you have pointed out many studies showed the vast majority of options (even in broad-based plans) went to the top 10 or so executives. In the end the FASB ended up with the disclosure requirement, but not mandatory expensing.

Delves: In your opinion is FAS 123 a "bad" accounting rule?

Leisenring: Actually I think it's one of the better ones. At least it put information in the marketplace that wasn't there before. You can't say it is terrible. It just could have been so much better.

Delves: As the FASB and the IASB move forward with option expensing rules, there are still major opponents. But it appears that the debate is far healthier this time around, compared to 1993 through 1994. And many companies have already said they would voluntarily begin expensing options.

Leisenring: Hopefully, now they will engage us in a measurement debate. I'm more than willing to change the measurement if you tell me that it's better. That doesn't bother me at all. That could be healthy and we may get a much better answer with that help.

Delves: All the minds need to come together on this. We need to talk about how we're going to measure this. But there are still some lingering arguments. What sort of things are you still hearing?

Leisenring: One of the arguments is that stock option expensing "double counts."

Delves: That argument says that the stock options are already reflected in the earnings-per-share calculation. If you then expensed them, it would be "double counting."

Leisenring: Some people believe that you can't put it in the denominator of EPS (earnings per share) and the expense numerator of EPS. But that's wrong. If you bought a truck with stock options, wouldn't you depreciate the truck? Or if you bought office supplies, would you not expense them? Would you pretend that you didn't use them? If you do use them and expense those office supplies, that's going to be in the numerator, and the two shares that you gave up for those office supplies are going to be in the denominator.

PART TWO

Elements of the Solution

CHAPTER FOUR

An Accounting Solution Everyone Can Live With

Whether to expense stock options has been the focus of a heated, widespread but ultimately narrow and limited debate. In reality this is a small point in a much bigger and more complex scenario. Now that it is finally widely accepted that there will be an expense, we can rightly turn our attention to several larger issues. These issues must be part of the real accounting solution that every company involved—Fortune 100 to start-up—can live with.

The larger, underlying concerns about stock options are encompassed in four broad areas:

- Options have been utilized in "one size fits all" incentive packages, which limit creativity and flexibility in executive compensation. As a result these incentives have been poorly designed and ineffective in helping companies meet their missions, strategies, and goals.
- Stock options are a perverse incentive, encouraging executives to take improper risks and to focus overly on short-term results. Options are supposed to make managers think and act like shareholders. Instead they make them think and act like option-holders, which is very different.

- Boards of directors are being asked to allocate ever increasing percentages of shareholders' future wealth to management. They are doing this with only rudimentary tools that compare their company's option grants with other companies'. The questions neither asked nor answered are: what do these options really cost the company and our shareholders, and what are we getting in return?
- For the past 8 to 10 years, a vast number of companies have hired people based on the false and unhealthy promise of "come to work for us and you'll get rich quickly." Instead of choosing a company based on its culture, products, people, and career path, far too many employees have joined a company based upon the gamble for quick riches. We are now living with the legacy of those decisions.

Because of our overreliance on heavy doses of stock options, America's compensation systems are seriously out of balance. As the vice president of human resources at a semiconductor company said, "Today we have employees all over the board in terms of compensation. Because we relied so heavily on stock options as compensation, we paid little attention to salary administration. Consequently we have inequities in the system, and we are not appropriately rewarding performance."

The solution to each of these problems is to adopt a multifaceted strategy, including:

- Determine and implement a mandatory expense for options—a solution that everyone can live with.
- Fully assess the true value of options—both the cost to the company and their perceived value to executives and other employees.
- Give boards of directors better tools for making decisions about options and other elements of executive compensation. To do that, boards have to start asking the right questions and demanding answers. In addition, company management as well as consultants must be far more thorough in providing information to boards.

- Make options much more performance-based. This means performance granting, performance vesting, performance-accelerated exercise prices, etc.
- Balance options with other incentive vehicles—and stock ownership. Create a balanced portfolio of incentives, which carries the desired motivation and risk profile.
- Rethink employee/employer contracts. What is the company giving, and what is it getting? What role do options play in the contract, if any?

In the next few chapters we will discuss each of these problems, their implications, and possible solutions. This is a vitally important exercise. As the Financial Accounting Standards Board (FASB) and the International Accounting Standards Board (IASB) seek comment and input on proposed rules, we must consider the implications of option expensing from every angle.

In this chapter we will discuss the first piece of the strategy, which is to design and implement a mandatory expense for options. As discussed in Chapter 3 we are fairly certain that the option expense under the proposed new rules will be based upon the fair value at grant date. But that alone does not present the framework of an expense that everyone can live with. Granted at this point it is more important to have expensing rules than to debate the issue for another 10 years. The logical next step is to move forward and implement an expense that, although it is clearly a compromise, will put an end to the notion that options are free.

ACCOUNTING RULE IMPLICATIONS

While we have defined the term "fair value at grant date" in Chapter 3, we have not examined the implications. What challenges will companies face as they implement those rules? What methodology should they employ? What is the right way to think about the costs and benefits of options?

To address these questions The Delves Group organized a conference in July 2002. Participants included members of the IASB and the FASB, Dr. Myron Scholes and other prominent academics, and corporate executives. The purpose was to consider accounting issues in depth, as well as the broader problems and potential solutions for stock options in general. Discussion at the conference focused on the total cost of an option, which includes two components. The first is the actual compensation expense. This is the value of the option at the time it is granted. This component would be expensed under the proposed new rules.

The second is the potential additional cost to shareholders of having to sell stock in the future at below-market prices. This additional cost would not be recorded as an expense on the income statement under the proposed rules. The reasoning is that Generally Accepted Accounting Principles (GAAP) do not reflect changes in the market value of most assets, particularly the market capitalization of the firm itself or its stock. Therefore, the argument goes, GAAP should not record the portion of the total cost of the option that is purely determined by the market.

Equally important to understand is that the expense will be fixed at the time of the grant with no subsequent adjustments, or "true-ups." There are two main reasons a company might want to adjust the expense after the option has been granted: change in price or change in assumptions affecting the initial value.

Despite this understanding of the option expense, there was a heated discussion at the conference about whether the grant-date expense should be "trued up" at a later date. Some participants were in favor of adjusting the original grant-date expense as more accurate information became available regarding the assumptions that went into the option-pricing model. The final consensus of the participants, however, was that the expense should be fixed permanently at the date of grant with no subsequent adjustments or "true-ups." I view this as a decision of expediency over accuracy.

The group also discussed the fact that the value of the options, and hence the grant-date expense, can be managed or reduced by changing the way the options are structured. Most performance features—such as tying the vesting date or the exercise price to performance—will lower the value and, therefore, the expense of the option. The reason is simple: when performance becomes a factor, the probability of a payoff from the options is lowered.

Interestingly companies looking to lower the potential expense associated with their option grants would be well advised to consider adding performance features and/or shortening the term of the options. However if performance-based options have a lower value, companies may also decide to grant more of them so that the net effect means no reduction in executive incentive packages. Nevertheless, fair value/grant date accounting points us in the right direction by providing companies an incentive (or at least eliminating a disincentive) to create more performance-based options.

Most importantly fair value/grant date accounting also would cause companies to examine the cost of options relative to the cost of other incentives. I hope this leads to more creative methods in executive compensation and incentives, and less of the "one size fits all" approach.

SPECIAL TREATMENT FOR START-UPS?

Another controversial issue raised at the conference, which deserves to be aired, is whether start-up companies need special treatment under the proposed expense rules. In preparation for the conference, I talked to some 25 CEOs and board members of Fortune 500 companies. Not surprising, their opinions in general were that (1) options do have a cost, (2) Corporate America probably has gone too far in allocating increased percentages of outstanding shares to executives through options, and (3) options should be more performance-based.

Interestingly, virtually every CEO and board member also expressed concern about the impact of option expensing on start-up companies. In particular they feared that start-ups would be hampered in their ability to attract and retain high-caliber people if option incentives carried a high associated expense. The ability of these start-ups to get their operations running would be severely diminished if they had to take an expense for the options they give to employees in lieu of cash.

When I raised this point at the conference, the panelists were virtually unanimous in their opinion. The panel's view, which reflected the opinion of the accounting rule makers, was there should be no special treatment for start-up companies. Their belief was that if a start-up can't make it on its own merits, then it shouldn't have any special treatment to make it viable. Another argument was that start-ups typically lose money; if the option expense (which is a noncash expense that does not impact cash flow) caused them to show a bigger loss on their income statements, what's a little more?

The option expense for start-ups will likely be so low that it's practically irrelevant and certainly not damaging. The viewpoint I heard from several venture capital firms is these are essentially cheap options on cheap stocks, worth maybe a nickel or a dime. So if the option exercise price is, say, 10 cents, the option expense is not likely to be any more than 5 cents per option. Even if a start-up grants an awful lot of them, the expense isn't likely to be overwhelming.

Another factor to consider in determining the right accounting treatment for start-up companies is that just as the stock in a start-up is different than a stock in a publicly traded company, so its options are different from those granted by publicly traded firms. On a technical basis, for options that are valued using Black-Scholes, a key assumption is a normal distribution of returns on the underlying stock (actually a log-normal distribution, to be precise). The distribution of potential returns on a start-up, however, is anything but normal. The payout can amount to nothing or it could be huge, with very little in between (a bimodal distribution, for all you statisticians out there). If we have to value a start-up's options as of the grant date, then we need to either utilize a different set of assumptions or use a different valuation model than we would use for an ongoing publicly traded company.

Beyond the technical points, there is also a big philosophical difference between the options granted by a start-up and those issued by a large publicly traded firm. For the start-up, options are used in lieu of cash. Simply put, start-ups usually don't have enough cash to pay people, so they issue options with the implicit understanding that the individual is willing to work for the promise of a future portion of the company's wealth. These options represent a significant gamble for the recipient, who doesn't know how much they'll be worth, if anything.

This is vastly different from the options granted by an established publicly traded company. In this case it's a pretty sure bet these options are going to be worth something. The options they grant are of an entirely different type. They are an incentive used by an established, ongoing concern. As we know from historic stock market performance from the 1920s through 2000, on average equities produce a 10 percent to 14 percent annual return over the long haul (bear market corrections included). An option granted by an established company has a far greater chance of turning into something than the options granted by a start-up.

Considering all these factors, I would argue that some provisions should be made for start-ups. Perhaps there is a "fairer" value for start-ups allowing them to postpone the recognition of the expense until some future date when the options have a more determinable value. The most appropriate valuation at some future point in time may be the intrinsic value of the options (the spread between exercise price and market price).

The Intel Argument

Another consideration with option accounting is that, by using it, we've created another noncash expense that has to be added back in order to determine cash flow and/or the economic value calculations at the company. Top executives at Intel, which has granted huge numbers of options to executives, middle managers, and employees over the years, rightly argue that expensing will likely result in another round of *pro forma* earnings calculations—that is, earnings before option expensing.

In a *Wall Street Journal* interview, Intel Chairman Andy Grove and Chief Financial Officer Andy Bryant assert that the current expensing fad could actually wind up making things worse. Bryant predicted, "companies will simply urge investors to look at earnings before option expenses—a move back toward nonstandard *pro forma* measures at a time when many companies are trying to shift to Generally Accepted Accounting Principles."

Technology firms that have large, unexercised option grants to expense aren't the only firms that will have trouble with fair value/grant date accounting. I spoke recently with the CEO of a large Midwest manufacturing firm whose stock has been basically flat over the past several years. His complaint was he holds options he has not been able to exercise. Taking an expense for these seemed like an absurd notion to him. "I have options that have never paid me a dime. Should the company have to take an expense for these? I don't think so," he remarked recently.

These arguments indicate the proposed rules may need to allow for expensing based upon either their intrinsic value when exercised or the "truing up" of the expense after the grant date. Perhaps companies should have a choice—expense now or expense later. Firms would then be able to expense based upon fair value as of the grant date (expense now), *or* they could utilize the intrinsic value or adjusted fair value at either the vesting or the exercise date (expense later). Under no circumstances would the question be "to expense or not to expense." Rather it would be how and when.

Seeking option expensing that everyone can live with, there is yet another consideration: whether stock options are also a liability and, therefore, a balance sheet item. Until now the proposed accounting rules and related discussion have been focused on the income statement (the company's net profit or loss). However, we must also consider options from the perspective of the balance sheet (the company's assets, liability, and owners' equity). Options would have to be considered on the balance sheet primarily as a contingent liability: the promise to deliver something of value in the future that is as yet undetermined but which must be estimated. This would be analogous to how pensions are treated on the balance sheet.

As balance sheet items, stock options would require actuarial assumptions based on stock price movements, probability of exercise, employee terminations, forfeitures, and future grants. It would also likely account for and include the impact of future potential cash inflows from the exercise of options, as well as the positive benefit of tax deductions related to option exercises.

In order for the balance sheet to balance, however, there must be an asset for every liability. If options are considered a liability, I contend that the corresponding asset would be an investment in human capital. Human capital represents the dramatically increasing value of human beings in the productive process. This is coupled with the fact that companies spend a lot for compensation and invest a great deal in the development and training of their people. The adage that "people are our greatest assets" is actually becoming increasingly true. For companies that sell services or software, all the value they create is from the human mind, as opposed to the conversion of raw materials into a manufactured product requiring vast amounts of physical and financial capital.

An example illustrated in Figure 4-1 shows that the fair value of the option itself would be included in owners' equity. Any positive spread between the fair value and the market value would be included in the liability section. The combination of those two components would be offset by an equal amount on the asset side, recorded as investment in human capital. Companies would then be required to earn a return on this investment.

Even before the latest round of FASB/IASB accounting rules, I saw the opportunity for companies to record stock options as a human-capital investment on the balance sheet. Let's say an executive is granted 1000 options with an exercise price of $10. Five years later, when the stock is trading at $100 a share, the executive exer-

FIGURE 4-1

Balance Sheet Chart

Including Stock Options as Investment in Human Capital

Assets		Liabilites and Owners' Equity	
Assets:		Liabilities:	
Cash	$	Accounts Payable	$
Accounts Receivable	$	Short-Term Debt	$
Investment in Human Capital		Long-Term Debt	$
Initial value of options granted	A	In-the-Money Spread on	B
In-the-money spread on	B	Unexercised Options	
unexercised options		Total Liabilities	$$
Gain on exercised options	C		
(net of tax)			
Total Investment in	A+B+C	Owners' Equity	
Human Capital		Paid-in Capital	$
Total Assets	$$$	Retained Earnings	$
		Initial Value of Options Granted	A
		Gain on Exercised Options	C
		(Net of Tax)	
		Total Owners' Equity	$$
		Total Liabilities & Owner's Equity	$$$

cises the options. If the options were accounted for as an investment in human capital, the transaction would be recorded as follows:

Debit	Credit
Cash +$10,000 (1000 share at $10)	Paid-in Capital +$100,000
Human Capital +$90,000	

Given the fact that the United States has a largely service economy, human capital has become just as important—if not more important—than physical capital. This has been especially true in computer software development, professional services, and Internet companies in which human capital may be the vast majority of the capital deployed. Because the people are the main asset of the company, a greater proportion of the value that is created should go back to the people who created it. This partially explains why these types of companies typically grant so many stock options. However these options should be recognized both as a cost and an investment in people.

A fundamental change has happened in the structure of American corporations, which needs to be recognized. Public corporations arose at the time of the industrial revolution out of the need to raise vast amounts of capital to fund enterprises like railroads, steel mills, power plants and public utilities. The public corporation was based on the capitalist philosophy and belief that the owners of a business provide money for the acquisition of physical capital (i.e., land, equipment, and materials). These were the main factors of production that a company invested in and the owners owned. The theory and practice was that owners bought physical capital, but "rented" labor. Labor was an interchangeable, replaceable, and fungible ingredient in the production process.

Today in technology and service companies this equation is reversed: human capital is truly the main investment. The problem, however, is that the industrial capitalist corporate structure does not reflect this. Stock options for all employees are an attempt to retrofit the needs of today's human-capital–based enterprise into the capitalist corporate structure, designed for industrial-revolution companies. Expensing options on the income statement—rather than reflecting them as human-capital investment on the balance sheet—is a continuation of old world, industrial revolution think-ing. Perhaps what we really need is a new type of corporate struc-ture that allows employees to become owners and reflects the new primacy of human over physical capital.

While the proposed stock option expensing rules are a big move in the right direction, how we come up with a solution that everyone can live with is still an open question. The fair value/grant date basis of the accounting rules will work for many companies. However, to do a thorough job, we need to decide what treatment will be given to start-up companies. If fair value/grant date is the standard for the options expense, then how will we adjust for the rest of the economic cost to shareholders of selling stock at below-market prices?

I believe that at least a portion of an option's economic cost belongs on the balance sheet—as a contingent liability *and* as a cor-responding investment in human capital. This concept must be given thoughtful consideration in determining an accounting treat-ment for options that everyone can live with.

WHAT DO YOU THINK?

- What is your company's attitude and position toward stock option expensing? Would you take the expense regardless of what other companies do? Are you relatively ambivalent on the issue, meaning that you'll take the expense when you have to? Or, are you adamantly opposed to the expense?
- Assuming stock option expensing is required, do you think the fair value/grant date measurement is the right answer? Do you know what the expense for your company would be using this method?
- Do you think the "spread" at the time the option is exercised is a better measure of the cost of your company's stock options?
- Do you think options really should be recorded on the balance sheet as a liability or contingent liability?
- Do you think there should be special treatment for start-ups, which use stock options in lieu of cash compensation?

BRIDGING THE GULF

The stock option debate is not just about the accounting rules and expensing. And yet that is where a lot of attention has been focused. On one side, you have all the companies that jumped on the expensing bandwagon at the beginning, but that did not do much to move the debate forward. On the other, there are the technology companies that oppose option expensing because they believe it is already factored into earnings per share. There is a gulf between these two camps that needs to be bridged. My interest is to further the debate and to allow all the viewpoints to be aired.

Ceridian Corporation, a leading information services company that serves the human resources, retail, and transportation markets, takes a hybrid approach to options and compensation. Ceridian uses options as an incentive and as a reward for executives and employees based upon performance. The company also requires its top executives to have significant stock ownership to align them more closely with both the ups and downs experienced by shareholders. Ceridian's Chairman, President and CEO Ronald Turner is generally opposed to an expense for options. However he believes that the question of stock option expensing is not "a matter of if, but when and how." He cautions that as the option expensing debate continues, there is no "one right answer" as to how they should be valued.

Delves: Tell me about Ceridian. What is its philosophy on executive compensation in general and options in particular?

Turner: The first thing is we have an extremely independent and active outside compensation committee and it's this committee that sets compensation with respect to the executive officers. Our baseline philosophy is that we will attempt to compensate the executives of Ceridian at the 50th percentile of the market. For the most senior executives a significant portion of their compensation is delivered in the form of stock options or restricted stock. If performance of the company is good, then that person can expect to receive compensation in the neighborhood of the 75th percentile of market. We do have a mixture of long-term incentives, which includes regular stock options and restricted stock.

Delves: What are you trying to accomplish with this compensation plan?

Turner: What we are trying to accomplish with compensation is putting our executives in the shoes of our shareholders as best we can, and to fairly compensate them. In addition to the baseline compensation program, our board has put in guidelines for each position that requires executives to acquire and retain actual shares—not just stock options. For example, for me, the stock requirement is five times my base salary, and for other senior executives it is two to three times their base salaries. Then not only do we have upside potential with the options but also downside potential because of individual stock holdings.

Delves: So you have a philosophy that executives should think and act like shareholders, and to do that you want them to own a sizeable amount of stock. Is that the main intent of the stock option program—to give executives an easy way to buy stock?

Turner: No. The main intent is to have a major part of their potential income—but not all—in the form of stock options. Options do provide the greatest leverage for the upside.

Delves: And with stock ownership, they have some skin in the game.

Turner: Exactly, it's a mixture of both. Below the top tier, we grant options to roughly 20 percent of our professional and management employees. Restricted stock grants are limited to the top tier of executives. But having those options in the hands of a large number of employees provides a broad base of people in the organization with an enhanced interest in what's going on with the stock market, and what is going on with the company in a macro sense—not just their particular area. It gives them a little bit of an eye toward the future, as opposed to the short term. It pushes everybody in the same direction.

Delves: If there is an expense, do you think you will likely change how you use options?

Turner: I think there is a reasonable probability that throughout the United States the expensing of options will reduce the number of stock options that are granted to a broader base of people in the organization.

Delves: Is that what you predict will happen at Ceridian?

Turner: Not necessarily. But we will have to look at the impact. It will get very deliberate consideration. I hope that doesn't happen. I think the intent of the changes was primarily oriented toward the top-level management. I think it would be unfortunate if it does reduce option grants to a broader base of people in the organization.

Delves: What is your opinion about expensing?

Turner: The issue is not whether to expense, but how much do you expense. By definition it will almost certainly not be the correct number. Thus what we have done is promulgated the issue of inaccurate accounting, which bothers me more than anything philosophically. The way that the system should work is this: You perform a deed or sell a product for which you are rewarded a value. And against that you charge costs. But this is one cost that has to be estimated, and it will never be an accurate reflection of the cost. Many stock options that are granted never materialize in any regard to the value that might be given to them in a calculation like Black-Scholes.

Delves: To me that is one of the drawbacks of taking the expense when the option is granted. This $10 option may cost me $100 or it may cost me $0. Should we record that when we don't know what the expense is? Or should we wait and see what happens, and therefore wait and see to take the expense. If it's zero, then it's zero. If it's $50, then it's $50.

Turner: What that does create, however, are unpredictable outcomes that are outside the confines of the normal operations of the company. There are many variables that influence the stock price, only one of which is the performance of the company. There are also market conditions, sector conditions, and operating conditions. All three could drive the stock price substantially. Many of us are now suffering from a macro impact, and many of our operations are more efficient than two to three years ago. But there are not many operations with a stock price that is higher than two to three years ago.

Delves: Another consideration in this debate is the treatment of stock options for start-ups. For many of these firms, options are an important component of their compensation in lieu of cash.

Turner: The higher the risk, the better options are as a mode of compensation. If you go to work for a blue-chip company and you do a good job, then under normal circumstances, if you want, you can still work for that blue-chip company in 10 years because in 10 years that company will still be there. But if you go to work for "Acme Internet" that has 12 people and an idea, it is a seedling in a forest of trees. It may or may not succeed. The probability of success is much lower, and the probability of you being with that company in 10 years is much lower than with a big company. I think stock options are a great form of incentive for that type of company. It doesn't influence the cash position from the get-go.

Delves: The options for a start-up are clearly very different than options in a company like Ceridian, and certainly different than options in General Motors or Sprint. They are different animals entirely. To tell me that I have to value an option for a start-up at the day of grant doesn't make sense to me.

Turner: Exactly. There is probably a 10 percent probability that a start-up is going to make it and really become worth something.

Delves: There are other approaches to option expensing. One is to determine the expense as of the exercise date. The other way to go about it is to determine the expense as of the grant date, but then allow it to be adjusted periodically as more information becomes available.

Turner: That may be a way to do it. But I believe all those things are going to have a tendency to draw the number of options down, because people who sit in my position and in my CFO's position next door, all universally get penalized for a lack of predictability and for variability.

Delves: Another factor to consider is that there is a difference in what the cost of an option is to the company, and what it is worth to the recipient. One of the reasons for that difference is that the options make the recipient's holdings undiversified.

Turner: And there is also a collegial spirit to hold options until closer to maturity, which means that these options are not really a freely exercisable instrument. And there are a lot of companies that have restrictions on the exercise of options and on the sale of any shares acquired. I know of a company that only allows options to be exercised once a year. The blackout period can easily be seven to eight months a year.

Delves: I believe that this is where the debate needs to happen, and we can get the academics involved in this. We can do a customized value for the cost to the company, and also a customized study of what the value is to the executive. If it does result in an undiversified portfolio, if there are blackout periods, what does that do to the value? There is a difference between the cost to the company and the value to the executive. If that's true, then what is the company getting for these options? Is it getting performance, esprit de corps, stock improvement, and so forth? That's the conversation I want to see people having at the executive level and at the board level.

Turner: It is an interesting dynamic. The most important thing to keep in mind in all of this is there is no one right answer on the expense or the valuation.

CHAPTER FIVE

Valuing Options

Many corporate executives, consultants, and even academics do an effective job of putting up a smoke screen when it comes to valuing options. Just mention the topic and you'll hear the protests that options can't be valued, Black-Scholes methodology results in values that are too high, and so forth. This smoke screen is nothing more than an attempt to cloud the issue of the inevitable accountability that comes with measuring the true cost of stock options and executive compensation. To clear the air for myself, I decided to seek the best advice I could find from two different camps that seem to understand options far better than most people: traders and economists.

The first group, traders, value options every day, including some long-term and complex option strategies involving both puts and calls. (A put is an option contract that conveys the right to sell a stock or other asset at a fixed price for a limited length of time. A call is an option contract that conveys the right to buy a stock or other asset at a fixed price for a limited length of time. An executive option is a call option.)

I took my executive stock option questions to Jon Najarian who has traded options on the Chicago Board Options Exchange (CBOE) since 1981 and who owns option trading and clearing firms in Chicago, including PTI Securities and Mercury Trading. With his goatee, ponytail, and brightly printed trading jacket, "Dr. J" is a familiar face on FOX Morning News. Like all professional traders, Jon has software programs at his fingertips. He scrolls through computer screens of short-term puts and calls as well as long-term equity anticipation securities (LEAPs). These are options with longer-term horizons from several months up to two years.

Professional traders use option-valuation models in trades they make for themselves and other speculators as well as for corporations trying to hedge highly complex risk. Some of these customized strategies are far more convoluted than executive options as we now know them. And yet these traded options and strategies are all evaluated using various option-pricing models. So what is the big deal about executive options?

When I posed this question to Jon Najarian, he had a very quick answer: it's no problem at all. In granting options to executives, all companies have done is "sold" call options in exchange for services. Granted executive compensation packages involve very large quantities of call options. But the sheer size of those grants doesn't make them any more complex than the offsetting or hedging transactions companies employ every day. In fact many corporations regularly hedge with tradable options to offset the risk of having granted so many long-term executive call options.

What this tells me is that sophisticated treasury departments, which manage the capital structure of the corporation, are very aware of the impact of these vast numbers of stock options granted. After all a company may have "sold" call options on 10 percent to 15 percent of the company in return for services from executives and employees. From a risk management and credit standpoint, this is a major-league transaction. It can't be shrugged off with the excuse that "gee, these options have no cost and no implications."

Not to trivialize the point, but ask yourself this: if you sold your neighbor an option to buy 10 percent of your house and property at its current market value, an option that could be exercised any time over the next 10 years, would you think of that as a meaningless transaction with no cost or value? Of course not. You have, after all, just sold 10 percent of the future appreciation of the value of your property. If you did that, you would at least want to receive an adequate return for it. You wouldn't just give away something of that magnitude.

Talking with a highly respected options trader like Jon, who deals with investors and corporate clients, was a valuable exercise. What I clearly saw was that valuing options—even those granted to executives—is very possible. Yes it does require its own brand of "rocket science" that must be programmed into valuation models. But what was once rocket science now is used in our everyday lives, from launching satellites to monitoring the weather. Similarly the figurative rocket science of option valuation can be applied to the day-to-day corporate world of executive compensation.

Executive options do have different characteristics than their traded counterparts. They have very long terms, usually 10 years; they have vesting requirements, during which time they cannot be exercised; many are exercised early once vesting is completed (often after five to seven years, if not sooner); and, of course, they cannot be bought or sold. In fact it is because executives can't buy or sell their options they tend to exercise them early. Despite all these characteristics, executive options can still be valued, taking all of these unique factors into consideration.

BLACK-SCHOLES AND BEYOND

Traders are certainly not the only ones who understand option valuations. Economists not only comprehend how to value options, but they have also developed, fine-tuned, and utilized many of the models in use in the marketplace today. Since I took a class in 1979 at the University of Chicago from Dr. Myron Scholes, I went back to him to ask about the valuation of executive options and the use of the model that bears his name.

When I reiterated the refrain of complaint that Black-Scholes valuations are too high, he laughed and said, "Absolutely not." I asked him if there should be some kind of discount applied to executive options because they are not tradable. Again his reply was, "Absolutely not."

"Remember," he said, "the object is to come up with the value of the option *to the company*—not to the executive."

The company can deal in its own stock and the derivatives of its own stock with virtually no restrictions. Therefore the value of the option to the company is not directly diminished simply because the person receiving that option cannot sell it. However the value of the option may be indirectly affected by the option's lack of marketability because executives will tend to exercise options early—that is, before the end of their 10-year term—partly because they cannot sell the option itself.

That points to the disparity between the value of the option to the company and the value to the individual receiving it. In general options are worth less to the employee than they are to the company. Just as any stock is worth more as part of a diversified portfolio than by itself, options are also more highly valued as part of a diversified portfolio. Options are highly risky derivative securities that should only account for a very small percentage of most portfolios. But even in the case of very wealthy executives, their option grants are often the single biggest component of their entire portfolio of assets. Their options outweigh everything else they have. Because of this imbalance, executives and employees tend to value the options they receive less than what they could potentially be worth.

As a dramatic example of this disparity in value, consider the experience of Centex Corporation. The company offered employees the choice of either receiving options or receiving 50 percent of the Black-Scholes value of the options in cash, which would be roughly 25 percent of the face value of the options. For example, if a $54 option had a Black-Scholes value of $27 a share, the company offered $13.50 a share in cash. "The overwhelming response was to take the money. A seven-year option is an enormously valuable thing to me, and yet people were willing to take 50 percent of the Black-Scholes value in cash, any day of the week. We had more demand than we had supply for," explained Centex Chairman and CEO Laurence Hirsch. (See Q&A interview with Hirsch at the end of this chapter.)

Centex's experience clearly shows that individuals valued the options significantly less than the Black-Scholes value to the company. "The thing that would have been interesting," Hirsch continued, "would have been if we said, now we're not giving 50 percent of the Black-Scholes value, we're giving 30 percent or 20 percent, and thus found the point at which the seller was neutral in terms of making a decision to hold or sell. But we never got to that point."

Another consideration in granting options to individuals is the concept that risk is a highly personalized thing. Even among people with similar salary levels, what is an unbearable risk for one person may be tolerable for another due to a variety of factors, from age to marital status to temperament. Another factor that enters into the value is the amount of direct influence employees or executives have (or believe that they have) over the stock price. If someone's performance is deemed to have a direct impact on the stock price, then that person will tend to value options more highly. If someone's day-to-day responsibilities have no clear or direct impact on the stock price, the options will tend to mean less to them.

Regardless of the circumstances, the fact remains that the very nature of options as high-risk derivatives tends to make them less valuable in the minds of people with undiversified portfolios. Thus a \$10 option may cost the company \$5 (reflecting the option expense), but it may only be worth \$3 to the person who receives it. Multiplied by the millions of options granted, this \$2 differential becomes significant. After all, the company is making a \$5 investment in something worth only \$3 to the recipient. Is the company going to get \$5 worth of return out of this investment?

These factors must be taken into consideration as companies move ahead with their compensation policies and strategies. Luckily for companies the real-world experience of option grants can be factored into the formulas used to calculate the expense. For example the fact an executive cannot sell or trade the options received can be accounted for in the variables or boundary conditions used in option valuation models. In other words the unique characteristics of the executive option (long term, not tradable, vesting requirements, and likelihood of early exercise) must be included in the variables applied to Black-Scholes or any other valuation model.

Let's say an executive receives options with a 10-year term. What typically happens is these options are exercised early, often after five to seven years. So this would shorten the term of the option from 10 years to five to seven years. Does that impede those options from being valued using Black-Scholes or any other model? No. It simply means the shorter effective term of the option must be accounted for in the initial valuation calculation. It's like the old joke about computing: garbage in, garbage out. In order for executive options to be valued fairly and accurately, the assumptions or boundary conditions plugged into the formula must be fair and accurate. If not, then the fault does not lie with the formula but with the inputs (or the person entering the inputs) to the formula.

Today there are numerous option valuation formulas, models, and methodologies. These include Black-Scholes and its variants, Binomial models, Trinomial models, Cox Ross, Gastineau, and so forth. Interestingly Najarian notes that when valuing traded options using these models, the calculations result in no more than a "nickel difference" in the valuations.

There is even something known as the "Coca-Cola method." The soft drink company, which grabbed the financial headlines in the summer of 2002 with its intention to expense options, came up with its own unique valuation method. Rejecting the option-pricing model approach, Coca-Cola said it would attempt to value its options by averaging solicited price quotes from two major investment banks. In other words the Coca-Cola method would seek input from the financial market to determine what the value of its options would be if these instruments could, indeed, be bought and sold. While this was an interesting idea, the investment banks ended up using option valuation models to determine their price quotes.

The applicability and accuracy of Black-Scholes is evidenced in its wide usage. As Dr. Jeremy J. Siegel, professor of finance at the Wharton School of the University of Pennsylvania and author of *Stocks for the Long Run* (second edition, McGraw-Hill, 1998) noted, "It [Black-Scholes] gave traders a benchmark for valuation where previously only intuition was used. The Black-Scholes formula was programmed on traders' hand-held calculators and PCs around the

FIGURE 5-1

Black-Scholes Option Pricing Formula

$$C = Sd^{-t} N(x) - Kr^{-t}N(x - \sigma\sqrt{t})$$
$$\text{with } x = [\log(Sd^{-t}/Kr^{-t}) \div \sigma\sqrt{t}] + \tfrac{1}{2}\sqrt{t}$$

S = current underlying asset price (in dollars)
K = strike price (in dollars)
t = current time to expiration (in years)
R = riskless return (annualized)
d = dividend yield (annualized)
σ = underlying asset volatility (annualized)

world. Although there are conditions when the formula must be modified, empirical research has shown that the Black-Scholes formula closely approximates the price of traded options."[14]

The Black-Scholes formula (and most other option pricing formulas and models) looks at the current stock price, the exercise price of the option, the time to expiration, the risk-free interest rate, the dividend rate on the stock, and the volatility of the underlying stock. Of these assumptions, the most important is volatility, meaning the swings or variation in price of the underlying stock. In general the more volatile a stock, the more likely it is that the market price will rise above the exercise price and the option will be "in the money." Figure 5-2 shows that the greater the volatility of the underlying stock, the greater the value of the option.

For the nonmathematician, a formula like Black-Scholes may look daunting. But that is not a reason to discount it. The fact is formulas, daunting or not, do exist and are used daily to evaluate options and complex transactions using options. It's not enough to say something is difficult and therefore can't be done. This is clearly a case of "the Emperor has no clothes, but no one wants to admit it." There is an entire body of knowledge, as well as decades of practice, in option valuation, which can be adapted for use in calculating the

FIGURE 5-2

Black-Scholes Assumptions and Relations to Option Value

Stock Option Estimated Fair Value

	Effect on Option Value	
Controllable Assumptions	If Assumption Increases	If Assumption Decreases
Expected Life of Stock Award	↑	↓
Risk-Free Rate	↑	↓
Exercise Price	↓	↑
Dividend Yield	↓	↑
Noncontrollable Assumptions		
Volatility of Stock	↑	↓
Market Price	↑	↓

value *to the company* of the options it grants (as well as the value to the employee, which is probably lower).

THE FOUR GUIDING PRINCIPLES

As we move toward more accurate evaluation of the cost of options, I invite companies to follow the Four Guiding Principles for Evaluating Executive and Employee Stock Options. All the implications of each point may not be known at this time. Nonetheless the criteria serve as a powerful guide to more accurate and responsible evaluation of the costs and risks involved in option grants.

Four Guiding Principles for Evaluating Executive and Employee Stock Options

1. Use the correct mathematics.
2. Input the correct assumptions or boundary conditions.
3. Consider options both as an expense and as a contingent liability.
4. Acknowledge that options are an investment in human capital, and calculate a return on that investment.

Let's take a look at these principles one by one.

1. Use the correct mathematics. There is a very sophisticated, robust science dedicated toward option valuation. The financial services industry knows how to apply it, as do numerous academics and economists. These mathematical formulas have simply not yet been applied thoroughly to executive and employee options.
2. Input the correct assumptions or boundary conditions. Using the right assumptions in the option methodology will require companies to take an actuarial approach. Given all the options it grants, what is the percentage that will be exercised early? What percentage will be forfeited? What percentage will never be exercised for whatever reason? How does stock performance affect the timing of

option exercises? Just as an insurance company studies the demographics of large populations to make assumptions about incidents of accident or illness and life expectancy, companies can apply this approach to option grants. Companies already have years of actual experience with which they can make assumptions and predictions, based upon things such as the age, sex, salary level, and years of service of the option-holder population.

The Delves Group, in partnership with Chicago Consulting Actuaries, has developed a comprehensive economic model to determine the "total economic cost" of options. For example what assumptions and predictions can be derived from the previous experience of companies when it comes to early exercise of options that would impact their value? What are the impacts on cash flow and EPS?

The better the assumptions used in the valuation model, the more "fair" the fair value of an option will become. This is of vital importance to major corporations, which might be looking at an option expense of $200 million to $300 million *per year*. The quality and accuracy of the mathematical model and inputs to the model could potentially save *tens of millions of dollars* per year in expense.

3. Consider options both as an expense and as a contingent liability. As mentioned in Chapter 4 and as I'll explore in detail later in this chapter, options should be thought of as a liability on the balance sheet with an offsetting investment in human capital. This will also be a complex actuarial determination no less important than the magnitude of the company's pension expense.

To do this accurately, companies will have to look at the actual experience of options granted in the past. For example, after what percentage increase in the stock price do people tend to exercise their options? As depicted in Figure 5-3, companies will most likely construct their own bell curve of experience, looking at the percentage

F I G U R E   5-3

Frequency Distribution of Stock Option Exercises versus Stocks Price Increase (Sample Company)

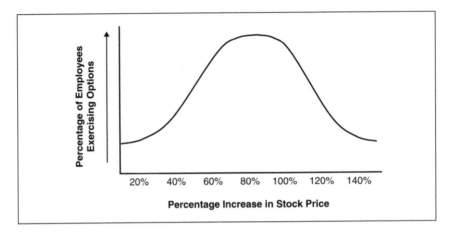

of employees who exercise their options after a certain increase in stock price and/or after a certain period of time.

4. Acknowledge that options are an investment in human capital, and calulate a return on that investment. This represents a philosophical shift for many companies. This also requires that companies look far beyond the option expense taken on their income statements. Instead they can also view these grants from the perspective of the balance sheet. This will require, as we'll discuss later in this chapter, options to be considered part of the capital structure and funding of the company, with all the risks and risk management that it entails. As with any other investment, an investment in human capital must produce a return.

Principles 3 and 4 take option evaluation beyond the realm of the accountants whose main concern is the expense issue. Viewing options as a contingent liability and an investment in human capital brings these grants under the purview of the corporate finance and treasury departments. Large companies have highly sophisticated corporate treasury and finance departments that understand the complexities of option valuation and the need to mitigate risks that result from option grants (as well as a host of other risks and capital structure issues).

THE PURPOSES OF STOCK

For the sake of perspective, let's take a brief look at the purposes of stock. The first is to raise capital for use in the business. The second is to provide a cushion for the company to offset the risks of running a business. If there were no risks, then a company would have no need to issue stock; a company could finance itself 100 percent with debt, which wouldn't require the company to share any ownership. Because of the risks involved, however, the capital received in a stock transaction is more than just a loan. It is an investment in ownership and a share of the future growth of the company.

Similarly if a company decides to grant thousands of call options on its stock, this adds another variable in how it has chosen to finance itself. The option grant commits the company to sell a portion of its stock at a fixed priced over a specific period of time in the future. A company may simply choose to live with that decision or it may seek to offset or hedge that transaction in some way. Hedging may involve buying back some of its stock at the prevailing price and keeping these shares on reserve as treasury stock. A company might also offset the options it grants by buying call options on its stock. Let's look at a simplified example. If the company grants 1,000 options with an exercise price of $10 ("selling" call options in exchange for services), it can then buy 1,000 call options with an exercise price of $10 in the open market. In this dynamic hedge strategy, when the executive exercises a portion of his or her options at $10, the company also exercises a portion of its $10 options. The risk and the cost to shareholders are then neutralized.

Another strategy companies frequently employ is to take the capital that would have been used to buy stock or options in hedging transactions and invest it in the business. If the company truly believes its performance could double or triple in the next several years, then it may decide that investing this capital in the business will likely produce the highest possible return. Or the company could pursue a combination of these strategies. Whatever the decision, the company must recognize when granting options that it has taken on significant risk and significantly altered its capital structure and financing strategy.

What it all boils down to is risk management. When a company grants options on 10 to 15 percent of its stock, it becomes a major-league risk management issue. It makes sense then that the CEO and the board of directors should look at this issue from a risk-management perspective. Shouldn't this prompt the board to seek answers on why the company is engaged in such a risky transaction as granting a significant portion of the company's stock (and future growth) in return for services? Wouldn't the board want to know how the company is being protected against this risk, and demand details about the return the company is getting for taking on this risk? To our collective chagrin this has not been happening. What's been happening is nothing less than bad corporate governance.

To be most effective, accurate, and responsible, companies must take the broader perspective of how options are used, why they are used, and what gains are realized from them. Luckily a vast body of knowledge can be applied to these tasks, from valuation models to actuarial calculations. Talking with people from human resources, finance, corporate treasury, options trading, mathematics, and economics, one can get a variety of different points of view on the subject. Now these disciplines must be brought together to develop and implement an accurate and workable means of valuing options, determining the cost and risks to the company, and recognizing the depth of this commitment and investment in human capital. The logical question then is what return does the company expect from this investment? Those who should be asking the question are the boards of directors. But to do that effectively, boards must be equipped with the right questions—and the right tools to evaluate the answers.

WHAT DO YOU THINK?

- Assuming you, as an individual, have stock options, what do you think they are worth to you personally?
  How big a portion of your net worth is made up by stock options?

In what ways have your stock option holdings influenced your attitude and behavior?

- What do you think stock options are worth to other people in your company?

    Do you think there is a difference in perceived value depending upon: the level or position of the person; the quantity and frequency of options received; or their previous experience with stock options?

- Assume the cost of an option to the company is 30 percent to 50 percent of the exercise price (if the exercise price is equal to the market price on the grant date).

    Do you think the cost to the company exceeds the value perceived by most executives and employees?

- How do you think options influence the decisions, behaviors and risk orientations of the executives who hold them?

    Do you think that large quantities of options cause executives to be more inclined to take greater risks? If so, do you think that is a problem?

- What do you think is the most effective way to motivate executives and managers to take appropriate risks that are in the best long-term interest of shareholders?

THE TRANSITION TO EXPENSING OPTIONS

There are several solutions to the problem of how to expense stock options. Valuation models and formulas are part of the solution. The next question to ask is then how to make the transition to expensing stock options. Let's take a look at a company that has done just that.

Centex Corporation, a nearly $9 billion, Fortune 500 company traded on the New York Stock Exchange, is a leading U.S. building company. It has operations in home building, home services, financial services, contracting and construction services, construction products, and investment real estate. In early 2002 Centex made the decision to expense stock options as part of its overall compensation philosophy. I discussed this change with Centex Chairman and CEO Laurence Hirsch at his office in Dallas.

Delves: What prompted you to decide to take the expense for options?

Hirsch: This decision was the result of years of frustration that options were not being properly valued by our management when evaluating long-term compensation programs. This was a free ride really, which resulted in a misallocation of corporate resources. It was "uneducated granting." All I know is options are worth something. If we went out today and said, "We want to give somebody options to buy Centex stock at the current price with a certain vesting schedule associated with it," then somebody would pay us for that option. I don't know what the number would be. But somebody would pay for that option, so clearly it has a value. If you are not evaluating or expensing stock options in any way, you're getting a dislocation in terms of decision-making.

Delves: Your decision to expense stock options then requires you to look at these incentives in a new way. Options are not just something that's "free" that could be readily given away, but rather an incentive that has to be evaluated within the context of overall compensation.

Hirsch: Exactly. For example how would you compare the value of a unit, such as restricted stock, to an option? What multiplier would you use, given the fact that with restricted stock or a deferred unit, you've got something "real"? A stock option, however, is only as good as the appreciation of the stock after the grant date. Now tell me what is the valuation based on that? Is it three options for one unit? Four options to one unit? Is it one to one? What do you think is the right comparison? Until now, that didn't matter because we weren't paying for options the way we were for other forms of compensation. But expensing options or figuring out some way to value them within the compensation system forces you to make that comparison. You have to decide how each is compared, and decide how the customer—in this case the individual employee—will value these various compensation instruments both in terms of perception and reality. That doesn't happen unless you somehow put a value on the option.

Delves: The decision to expense options is part of a larger compensation philosophy that includes, among other things, paying for performance with specific targets that must be met not only by the corporation but each of its divisions.

Hirsch: We've come up with the correct compensation policy for the entire company, which has been disseminated to each of our divisions. It focuses on two things. First, we emphasize that the pillar of our compensation is performance-based metrics. Second, once we determine our own internal metrics, we test them to make sure that they're market-driven so that our rewards are properly calibrated with our peers. Finally, we want to make sure that our programs really do align us with the interests of our shareholders.

Delves: How does this work within a framework of a decentralized organization, in which the divisions are each responsible for their own expenses, operating margins, and so forth?

Hirsch: The divisions are awarded options based on meeting specific performance targets. Once we are expensing options, that means whatever metric we have established—whether it's a metric based on return or operating margin or whatever—then everyone in the company and each of the divisions knows what targets qualify for an award. In addition to having to hit those numbers, the divisions know they have an additional expense to put into the formula, which will impact their annual cash bonuses. They have to be sure that they want to be granting options as incentives, and they have to be clear about how much they want to do.

Delves: This forces another discipline on the divisions. They're not just getting "free money" through options.

Hirsch: Absolutely. Our corporate center compensation is now generally based on growing the earnings of the company, whether it's 15 or 20 percent a year, whatever we decide is the right number, and giving certain returns on equity. We have to take a look and decide the impact of all these long-term plans, including stock options, on the ability to hit those numbers. So this runs both up and down the organization.

Delves: You have made expensing stock options a very real issue, at the corporate level and at the business unit level, since the business units are being charged for the options that they grant.

Hirsch: This is a very real issue. Let's say we now have 3 million shares more outstanding than we had prior to the issuance of options.

That's 3 million shares at $45 a share or so. Obviously people paid something when they exercised the options, plus we got the tax deduction based on the difference between the exercise price and the market price. So the actual cash outlay from the company's stand-point is net of the exercise price plus the tax benefit. Nevertheless we've got additional shares outstanding, and if we want to go back to the same numbers, we'd have to buy in that stock and put out the additional cash necessary to eliminate the dilution.

Delves As a result of executive pay over the years, companies have essentially written call options on 10, 15, or 20 percent of their equity. This is not a trivial event; it is very significant. The questions then become, what are the real costs associated with options? What is the economic consequence of having all these options in the hands of executives and employees?

Hirsch: My question would be have the options been an appropriate incentive to positive behavior that is equal to the overall cost of the option? I don't believe, as some pundits have said, options have been an incentive for bad behavior. I'm talking about has it been an incen-tive for good behavior on a one-to-one basis. I'm not sure they have. Part of it is the fact that the stock has not performed in accordance with earnings growth. I still believe that for most people, utilizing specific, controllable metrics is the best way to design compensation programs. To the extent that there are so many external forces that impact the price of the stock, you cannot necessarily relate perfor-mance solely to share price. That direct link is a little more tenuous. That doesn't mean that options shouldn't be granted. It does mean that there may be other as effective or more effective ways to com-pensate people than through the granting of stock options.

Delves: Having worked with Centex for a number of years, I know everything is very performance-based. People outside the company, however, may just see the high numbers for compensation but not the slope that leads up to it—or the fact that if performance drops off, pay drops off dramatically too. There is clearly a philosophy of performance-based pay here. Where did this come from?

Hirsch: It developed over time. I can't think of any specific moment in which we became a performance-based company. Looking back over the years, we always put some type of rules—like everybody else has—on various bonus plans. It made no sense to have all these plans that have performance hurdles, and then have stock options that have no performance hurdles. So it just came with the culture.

Over time everybody was pushed to be very exacting in determining compensation programs and to making sure that as part of that philosophy, there are significant pay differences among people performing the same function, based on their performances.

Delves: That is clearly what you've done. In divisions that do well, executives receive far more options than those in divisions that do not do well.

Hirsch: There is substantial differentiation between a poor performer and an exceptional performer.

Delves: You spoke about the pillars of your compensation philosophy. Tell me more about them.

Hirsch: The three principles are to be performance-based, market-driven, and aligned with shareholders. We explain the principles to be used in designing compensation programs—the questions we are asking them and the criteria they have to satisfy.

Delves: How has that played out?

Hirsch: My compensation, for example, is paid out 85 percent on financial metrics and 15 percent on nonfinancial metrics. Our plan basically maxes out this year (2002), for instance, based on financial metrics of 20 percent growth in year-to-year earnings and a 20 percent return on equity. It moves down very rapidly if those numbers aren't hit. That's for the bonus, and the options work the same way. We also look at a lot of other metrics—total operating margin of the company, among other things—to make sure that we are aligning the corporate metrics with the operating company metrics. And, we keep coming back to the primary thing that corporate managers should be responsible for: growing earnings and giving an appropriate return on equity to the shareholders. We've never linked it to stock price. While we're responsible for the stock, there are so many other external forces that impact it—many more than simply growth of the earnings.

Delves: Thus your metrics are based on what you can deliver to shareholders and what you can control.

Hirsch: Right. That's consistent throughout the company. All of our plans on the division level are based on what is controllable. One of the things that we got rid of 15 years ago was a lot of allocations that forced services and expenses on the operating companies. With performance-based plans, there should be a concomitant commitment that operational people should only be responsible to pay for what they can control. They should be in complete control of the factors that determine their incentive compensation.

Delves: What do you think are the major strengths and weaknesses of the program?

Hirsch: I think the strengths of the program are clear: We can use our compensation plans to appropriately align management's incentives with the interest of shareholders. The negative is that sometimes, to me, when it comes to setting targets—which is what we do—you can overdo it a little. Because of the drive for annual targets, you end up at times having people who don't invest in more dramatic process improvements. If we say that we want to grow the operating margin incrementally by 100 basis points or 50 basis points a year, then that can be achieved by honing the existing processes better. That's certainly a good thing, versus our competition. Good, solid, controllable, and sustainable growth. But this is not necessarily process-oriented thinking. Our compensation plan can limit leaps in corporate performance.

Delves: How would you do it differently?

Hirsch: I'm not sure. It would also have to be the result of a decision, for example, to increase margins by four points in a year. Then we'd have to realize that it would cost us a lot of money to retool the system. You would be more likely to do that during a weak time than during a strong time. During a strong time you're going to try to take advantage of the existing market, and you're not going to say, all of a sudden, "I want the whole system retooled."

Delves: So if you had to do it all over from scratch, there wouldn't be any major changes?

Hirsch: I'm very satisfied with where we are in the process. You have to be realistic enough to know that the system you put in place has a certain half-life to it, and you have to retool the compensation—not necessarily retool the company. We have a philosophy that we sunset every plan after three years, so that it gets a complete relook. Our people know that we're not going to pull the rug out from under them if they are doing much better than everyone expected. They have that three-year ride based on meeting and exceeding the objectives that we set. But after those three years, we shut it down, take a look at it, and see if we need dramatic changes in the system.

Delves: That's critical because people know what their game is—and they know that the game isn't going to change unexpectedly. Thus they can focus on operating margin improvement, or whatever the emphasis is in the plan. Is the focus, however, always on internal metrics?

Hirsch: We have done very well utilizing our internal metrics as the key components of our compensation system. Then in a growing economy, we were hitting our internal metrics, but those internal metrics were no longer completely in sync with external metrics (i.e., competitors' performance improving faster than ours). So we decided we have to look at every benchmark we have, decide which are the key ones, and then have a system in place to make sure we are setting our own internal metrics to exceed every external metric.

Delves: Do you have specific external metrics in your plan?

Hirsch: Yes and no. A decision was made not to put external metrics in the plan itself. We didn't want to do what some other companies have done, which is to say you've had a great year, but so did Companies X, Y, and Z—and they outperformed you. So we're going to take your compensation down. Nor do we want to say that the other companies did lousy this year because they had some problems, and because of that you're going to mint money. That reduces the certainty to the plan, and it significantly dilutes the effectiveness of the plan. We understand where our competitors are going. We set the right targets in relation to our competitors for each year.

Delves: If and when a downturn comes in your industry, how are you going to manage the compensation system, in terms of setting goals and objectives for people?

Hirsch: We'll have to evaluate it at that point, but we cannot move off our basic philosophies that we have put in place. If we are going to have a performance-driven plan, then we must have the strength of our convictions and in spite of what happens, we have to expect reduced compensation during downturns just as we expect higher compensation during the upturns.

CHAPTER SIX

Providing the Right Questions–and the Right Tools–for Boards

Over the past two to three years, board members have grown increasingly uncomfortable with their role as overseers of executive compensation programs. Given today's business environment, these feelings of unease are understandable, and they are expected. In private, candid conversations, many board members have begun voicing concerns that something is wrong with executive compensation—and that something frequently has a lot to do with stock options. Board members have seen executive pay grow at astounding rates as they approve ever-increasing allocations of stock— along with higher percentages of future shareholder wealth.

More and more corporate directors have admitted their concerns about the lofty levels of executive compensation. Perhaps, some admit, it has gotten out of control. Many of these board members are themselves CEOs and former CEOs who have had significant salaries, bonuses, and incentive rewards. What I find most interesting is that this questioning of the current state of executive compensation is not coming from the usual ranks of dissenters, such as unions and social activists. The criticism is coming from within the corporate elite. These successful, seasoned, and wealthy board members have the unique perspective to ask when enough is enough.

Among the voices of reason and concern among board members today is Warren L. Batts, an adjunct professor of strategic management at The University of Chicago Graduate School of Business and the retired chairman and CEO of Premark International. He has served on the boards of several prominent companies, including Allstate, Cooper Industries, Sears, and Sprint, and is an active and outspoken board member of the National Association of Corporate Directors. We spoke about the views of corporate directors on executive compensation, particularly as it relates to the granting of stock options.

Warren's concerns about options can be summarized in two main points. One is that options have a cost. What the exact cost is may not be determined at this point, but they absolutely have a cost. The second point is that options should be performance-based. He is concerned options do not really pay for performance and, in particular, they often provide significant rewards for low performance.

Warren has been forthright and thoughtful about the need for change to improve board governance and to make better decisions about executive compensation. His viewpoints are representative of a great many mainstream corporate board members, who clearly do want to pay for performance. Unfortunately board members do not currently have enough independent metrics and tools at their disposal to guide their compensation decisions. The main tool they have is competitive practice.

BOARD MEMBERS' CONCERNS

Adding to the compensation dilemma are two main concerns that face board members today. The first is overhang, which is the percentage of company stock dedicated to options. It has increased on average from 3 to 5 percent to between 12 and 15 percent—and significantly higher than this in technology companies. The overhang problem has resulted directly from the fact that there was no expense for options, and therefore no checks or balances on the system. Stock options, as a part of executive compensation, have grown by as much as 40 percent per year over many of the past eight to ten years.

The overhang issue is compounded when a company also has a large amount of options that are "underwater," meaning that the current stock price is far below the exercise price. This perplexing issue, which I call the "double bind," is addressed in Chapter 7 but is mentioned here because it is a critical issue for boards.

Some astute members of the media have also latched onto the overhang issue as far more worrisome than the expensing debate, which is "just a matter of accounting," according to CNN/Money Contributing Columnist Adam Lashinsky.[15] "The more interesting figure is the so-called options overhang or the potential dilution if all a company's outstanding employee stock options were exercised and sold. When that happens, the shares outstanding increase, and all things being equal, the value of each previously held share goes down," he wrote.

The second main concern facing boards is increased investor and regulatory scrutiny. The passage of the Sarbanes-Oxley Act of 2002 has exponentially heightened the regulatory awareness surrounding corporate governance issues. Waves of investor scrutiny are increasing in intensity. The Council of Institutional Investors and Institutional Shareholder Services have dramatically heightened their calls for increased disclosure. In fact the council was one of the first organizations to call for option expensing in early 2002.

While significant in and of themselves, these two concerns are symptoms of a deeper problem: how well are boards doing in truly paying for performance? When it comes to compensation, how much is enough, and how much is too much?

Clearly the current methodology of measuring, analyzing, and determining corporate compensation is not sufficient, according to Brenda Barnes, a former president and CEO of PepsiCola North America, an active member of several corporate boards, and an adjunct professor of management and strategy at Northwestern University's Kellogg School of Management. She argues that human resources departments and compensation consultants cannot simply confine themselves to competitive data in determining how much executives are paid. Companies and their boards must have a better methodology to determine appropriate pay levels, based upon responsibility, performance, and results. It's not enough, Barnes argues, to just look at *how* executives are paid; we must do a better job of answering the question of *how much* they should be paid.

My purpose in this chapter is to address these issues and to determine how boards can do a better job of analyzing, understanding, and making decisions about how and how much people are paid. Later in the chapter we'll look at some of the underlying philosophical issues that result in how executives have been paid.

THE TYRANNY OF COMPETITIVE DATA

Corporate boards of directors, human resources departments, and compensation consultants have done a thorough job of analyzing competitive data and paying people according to that data. In fact they've almost been religious about it. Their reliance on competitive data, however, has resulted in a kind of statistical tyranny, holding even well-intentioned boards captive to a standard methodology.

Typically when boards make decisions about executive pay, they take several specific steps.

- Hire a compensation consultant to help analyze competitive pay practices and provide insight into what other companies are doing. In the vast majority of cases, the consultant is hired by management to advise both management and the board.
- Gather competitive data. Management participates in numerous competitive surveys that consist of hundreds of companies and thousands of positions, with data including salary, bonus, and long-term incentives. This information provides a tremendous amount of detail about compensation across a broad spectrum of companies.
- Analyze the data, according to industry groups or according to size. The information can be sorted in a variety of ways to find out, for example, what people in specific positions are paid in a particular industry or in a particular size and category of company.
- Compare compensation practices with those of peers and with the broader market of all companies. In particular companies want to see how they measure up compared with the median and the 75th percentile. With this comparison, a company can see where it ranks in

terms of salary, bonus, total cash compensation (salary and bonus), and long-term incentives (mainly stock options), and the entire total compensation package.

The purpose of this whole process is to determine if the company is competitive in all areas of compensation and in line with its own compensation philosophy. For example a company may state it will pay at a certain level relative to a specific group of companies or type of company for salary, bonus, or long-term incentives, such as the median for salary, 60th percentile for bonus, and 75th percentile for long-term incentives.

Admittedly this all sounds pretty logical. However there are three main problems with this approach. First of all no one wants to pay below the median, with a few exceptions. There is an inherent and obvious problem with the quest to be above average. As more and more companies try to pile on top of the median line, the level changes. Companies increase their compensation to pay at or above the median, which raises the median level. The companies that fall to the bottom half (and by definition half the companies must be below the median) then try to leapfrog above the median again.

The second problem is how these comparisons are made. Typically, when a company is doing a competitive analysis of its compensation, it looks at data from companies with similar revenues. For example a $500 million steel fabricating company would look at data from manufacturing companies with revenues between $300 million and $1 billion. In addition a company may do a single regression analysis, looking at the statistical relationship between revenue and pay, to determine a more precise estimate of the right pay level for a company its size.

While it all seems to make sense, there is something wrong with this picture. Companies are essentially paying based upon size and not performance. This is not because the people involved— board members, compensation consultants, or whoever—didn't know what they were doing. It's because this is how the data has been used.

Back in the 1980s when I was at the consulting firm Towers Perrin, we tracked 30 to 40 different pieces of data related to compensation and ran sophisticated analyses to determine which data correlated most closely with pay. The data we studied included several different performance measures, as well as years of service, level in the company, number of employees at the company, number of direct reports, and so forth. Unfortunately what we saw, year in and year out, was the factor playing the biggest role in determining pay level was the size of the company's revenue. The other factors were far less significant. Performance was always exceedingly low on the list of determining factors.

To illustrate, in the world of statistics, the R-square value of a particular variable is very important. In layperson's terms it tells you the amount of variation in one factor that is explained by the variation of another factor. In our compensation analysis the biggest R-square was revenue. In fact, revenue tended to have an R-square of 60 percent or better, meaning that revenue size explained 60 percent of the variation in pay. In statistics, finding one variable with an R-square of 60 percent is like unearthing the proverbial Holy Grail. When we added in factors such as experience and years of service, the R-square rose as high as 75 percent, thanks to the hefty influence of revenue size.

In the end we stopped doing this type of multiple regression analysis at Towers Perrin, in part because customers didn't want to pay for it, but also because it did not yield information that was particularly useful. We had hoped it would provide a better way to tie pay to performance. What it revealed, however, was reality: revenue size was the most influential factor in compensation. To this day the R-square value of revenue remains incredibly high in compensation. The way the competitive data is analyzed and used reinforces the relationship between company size and compensation.

The third problem with the traditional use of competitive analysis stems from the concept of "free" options. In cash compensation there is a natural limit to the tyranny of competitive data. Simply put, cash is finite. No matter how much a company might want to leapfrog to the top of the compensation pile, it is constrained by the available cash and the size of the expense. Thus companies generally limit themselves to 4 percent to 8 percent annual increases in salary for executives. Companies have shown a willingness to grant large cash bonuses but only if performance standards are met. Bonuses as a percentage of salary grew from 40 to 50 percent of a CEO's salary to 80 to 100 percent of salary throughout the 1990s. Recent studies are showing significant drops in bonus payouts as company and economic performances have fallen off. No such checks and balances exist for stock options, however. The leapfrogging effect of doling out bigger and bigger grants to keep up with the corporate Joneses has gone on almost completely unfettered.

Better Questions, Better Answers

Current compensation practices and the granting of vast amounts of options have brought us to where we are today. Now boards of directors need to take a more in-depth approach to compensation. They must ask better questions and must get better answers. They must be willing to make management and consultants uncomfortable with their questions. And they need to be persistent in asking questions for which there are no easy answers.

Boards can't be ruled by precedent and by what everyone else is doing. It is no longer acceptable for management and its consultants to say, "this is the way it's always been done." Changing will require boards to move out of the comfort zone of common practice. Boards typically seek the assurance that they are following the standard methodology and not deviating too significantly from the norm. In fact the reason most boards hire a compensation consultant is to know they are getting the standard answers on compensation in line with what other companies are doing. But this is a self-perpetuating problem.

The conservative behavior of board members preserves the status quo and discourages any approach that appears too risky. This is completely appropriate and is a large part of a board member's job. At the same time it promotes lemminglike behavior in which everyone wants to jump off the executive-pay cliff. In fact they seem to challenge each other to see which lemming can jump off the cliff with the most outrageous dive.

To change the status quo, boards of directors do not have to abandon what they've done (and done well) thus far. There is no reason to stop doing a thorough job of competitive analysis. But it should be the foundation of a more thorough study of executive pay against a variety of other comparative and competitive metrics. Specifically:

- Boards must take a multiyear perspective when it comes to compensation. This is particularly important with stock options, since they are not annual events but accumulate over time.
- Compensation must be examined relative to executive performance. This will require an analysis of changes in compensation relative to changes in corporate and individual performance as well as changes in performance over a multiyear time horizon. The purpose is to determine how executives are paid and how sensitive compensation is to increases *and* decreases in performance.
- The company's incentive systems must be studied to determine the impact of performance on compensation. This will help determine a company's "pay for performance score," showing how compensation varies based upon specific performance measures. The greater the variation in compensation due to performance the higher the pay for performance score.
- Conduct the same type of analysis for a peer group of at least 10 to 15 other companies. This will reveal how these companies' compensation practices have varied based upon performance. Using this peer analysis, a company can compare its pay for performance score to that of other companies.
- A company should also determine the pay for performance score for several different performance measures. This would include return on investment, change in profit, change in margin, change in shareholder return, change in revenue, and so forth. Once again comparisons should be made with the peer group.

This in-depth investigation in compensation forensics will provide a valuable historic perspective of what the company typically pays for—and how well it does in paying for those performance measures.

Option Pool Analysis

The next step boards must undertake is an option pool analysis. Although options are usually looked at as yearly grants, they are by no means annual compensation. Options motivate people in large part because of how many a person holds and the degree to which the options are in-the-money. Boards have to look at the total number of options held by an executive as well as that person's individual wealth sensitivity to changes in the stock price. The objective is to determine how paper wealth from the in-the-money options increases or decreases due to fluctuations in the stock price.

After the analysis is completed, boards need to review the option pools at other companies. To make a comparison adequately, they should look at the pool not only in terms of the number of options granted but also how far in-the-money they are. This "in-the-money-ness" of the options pool will yield an "option wealth sensitivity" score by which a company can compare itself with its peer group.

Once the option pool for each executive is determined, a "wealth transfer analysis" can be conducted. This analysis looks at how much wealth was transferred *on paper* from shareholders to the CEO and other top executives, both individually and as a group, for at least the previous three years. Projections can also be made showing how much wealth will be transferred in the future at different rates of stock price appreciation. Let's say an executive holds 100,000 options that are at or in the money. If the stock price goes up $10, a paper wealth transfer of $1 million results.

Compare the paper wealth transfer in any given year to the company's performance in that year. What is the correlation? Then what is the comparison with the paper wealth transfer at peer companies?

The next analysis is to determine the total cost of management at the company; in other words, what it costs to manage the company. This can be accomplished initially by looking at the salary, bonus, and incentives paid to the five highest-paid people at the company. The analysis should ideally be extended to take into consideration the CEO, the CEO's direct reports, and possibly the next level down. In one analysis consider the salary and bonus of the top executives as individuals and as a group. In another add in the cost of their options (and other long-term incentives) as of the grant date. The resulting total cost of management should be compared to a peer group of other companies. Weighing this cost against various performance measures will result in a return on management showing what the company is getting for what it pays.

Once the return on management is determined, a company can start to see the relationship between changes in profits and the total cost of management. Are the changes commensurate? If profits went up 15 percent, for example, did the cost of management go up by an appropriate percentage? How does that compare to other companies in the peer group?

Each of these analyses is possible with existing data. All that is required is the determination by boards to insist on more thorough analyses and to dig into one of the most critical issues in corporate performance.

TAKING A DEEPER LOOK

The subject of board governance with respect to executive pay, however, cannot stop at improved measurement and data analyses. It requires a deeper look at the role of the board itself. Looking at history, we gain a better perspective on this investigation. As discussed in Chapter 2, corporations owned by nonmanager stockholders started in the early 1800s but did not really become widespread until the Industrial Revolution. What distinguished these companies was that they were founded as corporations whereas before that time individuals or families owned virtually all companies. These new corporations were able to raise vast amounts of capital to fund ambitious ventures like building railroads, steel mills, and automobile plants. Through sales of stock, they had access to thousands, if not hundreds of thousands, of investors, instead of just a handful of people or family members.

Because of their complexity, these new corporations hired managers to run them. For the first time in history, there was a separation between managers and owners. This created a need for a strong board of directors, elected by the shareholders to oversee the activity of the hired management. What made the board of directors necessary was the realization that hired management couldn't always be expected to act in the best interest of the shareholders and owners. Human nature being what it is, the hired managers will act in their own best interest, which may not always be in sync with the best interest of shareholders. This continues to be a major issue today, requiring not only better executive compensation programs, but better governance and oversight.

Economist Adam Smith recognized this issue some 200 years ago in his seminal work, *The Wealth of Nations*. "The directors of such companies, however, being the managers rather of other people's money than of their own, it cannot be well expected, that they should watch over it with the same anxious vigilance with which the partners in a private co-partnership frequently watch over their own. Like the stewards of a rich man, they are apt to consider attention to small matters as not for their master's honor, and very easily give themselves a dispensation from having it. Negligence and profusion, therefore, must always prevail, more or less, in the management of the affairs of such a company."[16]

In the 1980s and 1990s economists Michael C. Jensen of Harvard Business School and William H. Meckling of the University of Rochester codified this phenomenon in their "agency theory," which looked at the basic conflict between shareholder/owners and hired managers. Jensen revisited and expanded the theory in the *Journal of Applied Corporate Finance*.[17]

"Agency theory postulates that because people are, in the end, self-interested they will have conflicts of interests over at least some issues any time they attempt to engage in cooperative endeavors," Jensen wrote. While these conflicts are evident in a variety of structures and cooperative endeavors, focus was placed on the "conflicts of interest between stockholders and managers in the public corporation, not only because of the vast extent of the resources now controlled by such organizations, but also because those conflicts of interest are obvious and easily observed in the world around us."

The purpose of executive compensation is to fix the principal-agent conflict by finding a way to align these corporate agents with the interests of the shareholder principals. The solution, as alluded to earlier in the book, was thought to be stock ownership. If people owned enough stock or were granted enough options, they would automatically act in the best interest of shareholders. Boards and management thought they had found a magic pill to cure the ills of the principal-agent conflict. If they gave out enough pills, then through the invisible hand of capitalism, everyone would be led to do the right thing—namely maximize shareholder wealth.

Stock ownership and stock options, however, are certainly not a magical solution to replace effective oversight and good management. Enhance it, perhaps, but not substitute for sound corporate governance. Capitalism being what it is, these incentives did sometimes cause managers to maximize short-term shareholder wealth by inflating the stock price. The means to that end, however, occasionally involved "cooking the books" or less devious ways of managing reported earnings.

I've rarely seen stock ownership and stock options alone create a better managed company. In fact maximizing shareholder wealth in and of itself is a narrow and shortsighted vision of a company's purpose. This is analogous to saying that, as a husband and father, my total value and success is measured solely by how much money I earn, the size of my house, and the type of cars I drive. While it is important and meaningful that I provide for my family, it's only part of the overall picture. It does not acknowledge the real, long-term value I bring to my family: the quality of our relationships, our emotional support and love for each other, the values we share, and the nurturing environment we create for individual growth and development.

The same is true for a corporation. We are all part of a society of human beings. As authors James Collins and Jerry Porras state so eloquently in *Built to Last*, the most enduring corporations have a clear purpose, mission, and set of values that transcend time and generations of leadership. Companies that are consistently strong in these areas also tend to significantly outperform the stock market.[18]

While shareholder return is an important measure, it is the result of effective oversight and good management. This is where the emphasis should be placed, instead of the single-minded quest for shareholder return by any means. The purpose of a firm is to maximize the benefit to all its constituents, including shareholders, customers, employees, the community in which it operates, and the environment.

Within this context what are the implications for boards of directors, with respect to their roles as supervisors of management and agents of the shareholders? They are:

- To attract and hire high-caliber management.
- To establish with management performance contracts that define clearly the mission and purpose of the organization, specific strategies, goals, and measurable results.
- To administer the contracts and hold management accountable to achieving these goals.

To fulfill these criteria boards must be prepared to take decisive actions. The first role, to attract and retain the best people, requires corporations and their boards to be willing to pay a lot for excellent performance—and to be willing to terminate poor performers. One of the biggest problems over the past 20 years in Corporate America has been a brain drain. Top talent out of business and law schools have shied away from corporations in favor of investment banking, consulting, and law. Not only could they earn more but these highly motivated people were paid based on performance. Thus they gravitated toward places where they could reap higher rewards—albeit with far greater risks—than the traditional corporation.

Corporate America, by and large, still does not provide adequate compensation to attract this talent. The exception has been stock options, although this is a completely inadequate answer to the problem. Boards have believed it was acceptable to grant options because they automatically produce high payouts through stock price appreciation, which would also benefit the shareholders. Now boards must have the courage to pay significant financial rewards for significant financial performance and also pay low financial rewards when returns do not meet specific requirements. The ultimate "low reward," of course, is termination, which boards have to be more willing to do and execute quickly. If the board giveth, the board also must be willing to taketh away.

Secondly, the link between pay and corporate revenue must be severed. This ludicrous pay mechanism has led to empire building, in which size seems to matter above all else. A better approach is for the board to look at the total cost of management relative to company performance in order to get a good return on management. This should then be compared with relative performance of other companies.

Thirdly, boards should limit the relationship between total compensation and shareholder return. While important, shareholder wealth creation is only one of several elements that should be monitored and rewarded. Other considerations at least as important include traditional financial measures such as profit, margins, and return on investment as well as marketing-oriented measures like market share and customer satisfaction.

It is important the board provide oversight of the culture and values of the company and the company's relationship with employees, the community, and the environment. It's been demonstrated over and over again that corporations with healthy cultures, solid values, and strong relationships with their communities engender loyalty, productivity, innovation, and long-term excess shareholder returns.

Healthy and responsible governance requires companies to take a step back to view compensation policies and practices from a new perspective. To do a more effective and more responsible job, boards have to move out of the comfort zone of competitive data and standard practice to devise compensation that offers potentially lucrative rewards for excellence.

WHAT DO YOU THINK?

- What do you think is the ultimate purpose of corporations in our society?

  How should we measure their success as corporate citizens?

  Is long-term total return to shareholders the ultimate measure of a corporation's success, or are there other criteria to be considered and rewarded?

- How does your organization articulate and manifest its mission and purpose?

  Is this clearly communicated to shareholders and employees?

Is your company's mission and purpose, along with its values and standards, incorporated into and reinforced by its compensation system?

- What messages are sent by your company's executive compensation system?

What behaviors and results are valued and rewarded?

Is individual performance valued over team performance or vice versa? Long-term performance versus short-term performance? Quantitative versus qualitative?

CHAPTER SEVEN

Making Options Performance Based

Companies are at a crossroads in terms of determining executive compensation packages. They will need to consider whether options will be a part of their compensation going forward, and if so, how they will be structured. To do this they will have to look at why options have been granted in the past, and the purpose they serve for the future.

When it comes to option grants in the future, companies will take one of three basic courses of action:

1. They will continue to grant stock options as they always have and take an expense to cover them.
2. They will stop granting options or grant fewer of them and replace them with some other incentive deemed more cost-effective.
3. They will make options more performance-based.

In this chapter we will examine this third strategy and explore performance-based options in detail. Before we move into the third alternative, let's take a quick look at the first two possible courses of action. With the first alternative—continuing to grant options and taking the expense—there are some situations in which options are a particularly useful compensation tool. For example start-ups and venture firms that do not have a lot of cash need to provide noncash compensation. Executives and employees at start-ups generally understand they are giving up at least a portion of their cash compensation in return for a less likely but potentially lucrative long-term payoff. Since the majority of start-ups fail—let alone go public and sell for big earnings multiples—there is quite of bit of risk associated with the options granted by a start-up firm. But as long as employees understand that risk, options can be an effective part of the compensation plan.

While options make sense for start-ups, I do not think they are the best compensation alternative in established, ongoing public companies—particularly when they are granted in large quantities. Up until now stock options have been granted in a way that has provided a lucrative reward for mediocre performance. Since stock options have been granted at-the-money (with an exercise price equal to the stock price), the stock price only has to rise slightly for the option to be worth something.

The second strategy—not to grant options—will require companies to utilize other incentives. For example companies may opt to grant some kind of multiyear, financial performance-based incentives. Smaller quantities of options may be used in combination with these other incentives. We will explore these alternatives in detail in Chapter 8.

WEIGHING PERFORMANCE-BASED OPTIONS

Making options more performance-based may be a viable strategy for companies wanting to continue granting options as an incentive for future performance. Given the expected change in accounting rules, it will be easier for companies to make options performance-based than it has been in the past. Under existing ("old") accounting rules, performance-based options were subject to variable accounting, which few companies wanted. The expected new expensing rules, however, would make it possible for performance-based options to be used without introducing undesirable accounting consequences. All options would have fixed-expense accounting regardless of how they are structured.

Most performance features added to options under the new rules would lower their value—and consequently lower the required expense per option to the company. If an option is only exercisable if certain financial goals are achieved (performance vesting), then the likelihood of that option being exercised is lower as is its value and required expense. As a consequence companies may increase the number of options granted so the total value of the package is not negatively impacted.

As much as performance criteria seem to make sense for option grants, companies must understand the impact of performance criteria on the perceived value of the options. When all is said and done, will companies and their executives look at performance-based options with enthusiasm or disdain? Will performance-based options provide the right incentive, or will executives say, "No, thanks. I'd rather have something a little more lucrative."

THE PURPOSE OF OPTIONS

The answer lies in the purpose of the option. As we move from the false notion of "free" options to expensed options, companies must ask themselves what the options are supposed to do. Once the company determines that, the choice of whether to offer performance-based options becomes clear.

Options have the potential to do three specific things:

- Provide the potential for executives and managers to accumulate wealth over an extended period of time that is tied to the long-term success of the company and particularly to the growth in the company's stock price.
- Provide an incentive to pursue specific activities or results.
- Provide an incentive to take actions that would cause the stock price to go up.

Starting with the first point, wealth accumulation, I remember back in the early 1980s when I was at Arthur Andersen, working as a financial planner for executives at firms such as Abbott Laboratories and Sara Lee. In those days before option mega grants were a twinkle in a CEO's eye, a typical mid-level executive over the course of his or her career could make $1 million to $2 million on options. Over the years the executives would build up a sizeable portion of options that would gradually be exercised. It basically amounted to a combination long-term incentive and savings/retirement plan all tied to company stock. In that way it was not unlike more traditional stock-based profit-sharing plans.

The option grants of the early 1980s also allowed executives to accumulate wealth over a period of five to ten years or longer. Despite the hype over mega grants and excessive compensation packages, the option plans of today can also serve a long-term savings function. Most stock prices don't skyrocket through the roof, allowing someone to exercise their $10 options a year or two later for a stock worth $100. Stocks usually go up gradually over time, thereby providing a means of long-term capital accumulation.

If the intention of the company is to allow executives and employees to accumulate stock via options for the purpose of long-term wealth accumulation, then it can continue to do that. Another alternative, of course, is for the company to increase its contributions to the 401(k) or pension plan. Or the company could give employees deferred or restricted stock. The company could also lengthen the vesting period on the options or require that shares acquired from option exercise be held for a minimum period of time. If options are to be used for wealth accumulation purposes, there is no need to attach performance criteria to them. However if options are to be used as an incentive to encourage certain goals or targets to be met or exceeded—then it makes sense to use performance measures.

ADDING PERFORMANCE MEASURES

There are many ways in which performance measures for options can be introduced. For our purposes here, we'll take a look at five different strategies that offer a variety of solutions, depending on a company's needs.

Basing the number of options granted on performance is a straightforward technique. The better the performance of the company or a particular division, the more options are granted to executives. The lower the performance, the fewer the options granted. If the performance fails to match a certain threshold, then no options are granted. This currently is the most common approach used. Many companies base the size of their annual option grants at least partially on individual or company performance.

Accelerating vesting based on performance is another performance-based alternative. Accelerated vesting options are used currently because they have zero expense under current accounting rules. For example a company grants a certain number of options that will vest at some time in the future, such as in seven years. If certain earnings or other financial targets are hit, however, the options will vest sooner, perhaps in three years. Options may also be subject to accelerated vesting if the stock price reaches or exceeds a certain level for a sustained amount of time.

Another alternative is to vest stock options only when performance targets are met. Here an executive is granted an initial number of options, say on 10,000 shares of stock. When the first goal is surpassed, 3000 options would vest; at the second goal, 3000 more options would vest; and then at the third goal, the remaining 4000 options would vest. If none of the goals were achieved by a specific time, three years for example, none of the options would vest.

Accelerate the exercise price. This solves the problem of options providing a lucrative reward despite mediocre performance. These options only pay out if the stock performs better than some specified minimum growth rate. There are several ways to do this. One way is to have a variable exercise price that increases by a predetermined percentage per year. Unless the company's stock performs above a specified minimum threshold rate of growth, the option is not in-the-money.

Another alternative is to increase the exercise price at a rate equal to the company's cost of capital. The cost of capital is the minimum rate of return a company has to pay to lenders and shareholders for the capital they provide. If the stock appreciation does not outpace the cost of capital, the option is not in-the-money.

Utilizing indexed options requires the company to outperform the market or a group of peer companies. With indexed options the exercise price moves up and down with the stock market. The exercise price is tied to an index such as the Standard & Poor's 500, the Nasdaq Composite, or a basket of stocks representing a specific group of companies. Whatever the criteria, the options would only pay off only to the degree that the stock out-performs the benchmark.

For example assume a company grants options with an exercise price of $10 when the stock is currently trading at $10. The exercise price, however, is tied to the performance of the stock market. If the market rises by 20 percent, then the exercise price becomes $12 a share. If the company's stock only goes up to $11 a share, the option is out of the money. On the other hand if the stock outperforms the market and trades at $15 a share, the option is in-the-money with a $3 potential gain. Consider what happens if the market (or the appropriate benchmark) declines by 20 percent. Then the exercise price is $8. If the stock were trading at $8 or above, the option would be at- or in-the-money.

However, indexed options do not completely avoid the problem of underwater options. What indexed options can do is ameliorate it. Even if the exercise price declines along with the overall market (or benchmark) the option would have value as long as it outperformed the market.

DEALING WITH UNDERWATER OPTIONS

As companies consider the future of option grants, many are also wondering what to do with previous option grants that are now underwater. Given the bursting of the Nasdaq bubble and the sharp declines in the stock market since 1999, many companies have 50 percent or more of their outstanding options underwater. In addition many companies find themselves in a double-bind situation where they have a high percentage of options underwater *and* a high percentage of overhang (unexercised options). Not only are most of their outstanding options potentially worthless, but they may also have a difficult time getting any more shares authorized for new option grants. This is becoming a common problem for small-cap companies whose stock price has dropped dramatically. They just don't have enough shares. What then should these companies do?

Admittedly it's hard to develop an objective philosophy when 80 percent of your options are underwater. It's better to have the philosophy ahead of time, stipulating what actions should be taken when a certain percentage of options become underwater. Nonetheless if companies have not developed a philosophy before and are now dealing with a large percentage of underwater options, they have two alternatives: reprice them or leave them alone.

In general, if the purpose of the option is to provide long-term capital accumulation, then options should not be repriced. Options in this case are granted year after year, and most likely over the long term, these options would accumulate some value. Thus if the stock price has gone down for a couple of years, resulting in underwater options, then so be it. The next few rounds of option grants should make up for the underwater options.

If the purpose of the options is to attract and retain employees, then some companies should seriously consider repricing their options. After all options are supposed to act as an enticement to attract and retain talent. With those options underwater, they have lost their "glue." A company may find itself at risk of losing good people because the vehicle it used to attract and retain them is no longer effective. There is no way these options can become "sticky" again unless some action is taken. Under the general umbrella of repricing, there are two basic strategies:

- Cancel the underwater options and reissue replacements with a lower exercise price. "Old" accounting rules require that these two events be separated by six months' time in order to avoid variable accounting (and retain fixed or "free" accounting) for the newly issued options. The new proposed rules would require the company to take an expense only for the newly issued options. The six-month separation between cancellation and reissue would no longer be necessary.

- Lower the exercise price on the existing options. This results in variable accounting under the old rules, and would likely be treated as a new option issue under the new rules.

An important issue for companies to consider, however, is the extent to which the options are underwater. Repricing should not be considered unless the stock price has gone down by at least 50 percent—and at least 50 percent of the outstanding options are underwater. I call this the $^{50}/_{50}$ rule, a general rule based on working with many companies considering repricing. A smaller decline in the stock price—or a smaller percentage underwater—can be made up over time with a recovery in the market.

There has been a lot written about the impropriety of stock option repricing and how it is a low-integrity act by companies and their boards. As Graef "Bud" Crystal, a former compensation consultant and outspoken executive-pay critic and columnist, puts it, if a company's stock is volatile enough and it is willing to reprice its underwater options on a regular basis, then it has created a virtual money pump for its executives. Perhaps a nice benefit to executives but not so nice for shareholders.

However, for the company that finds itself in a bad double bind—say with 80 percent of its options severely underwater and a 20 percent overhang—option repricing may be the only way to go. Like it or not, executives and managers can walk. They are their own transportable, transferable assets. Even if their options are not portable, they personally are. And they can get new options at a new company that are at-the-money and not underwater.

So if a company's options have lost their ability to retain people—and no new option shares are available—then the company may have to reprice some or all of its outstanding options or resort to another type of long-term incentive. In my mind there is no major sin in this, just an expedient solution to a difficult problem.

So when is it the right time to reprice options? Certainly companies can follow some criteria for when and how it's appropriate to reprice options. One criteria is the $^{50}/_{50}$ rule. As described above, if 50 percent of a company's options are more than 50 percent underwater, then it's probably time to at least consider repricing. This is particularly true if the company has no more shares to issue and a high overhang.

Another criteria to consider is if the repricing can be done on an approximate value-for-value basis. The company should calculate the Black-Scholes value of the underwater options and the value of the new "replacement" options and then make sure that the value of the new options is approximately equal to the value of the options traded in. This will usually result in two, three, or even four old underwater options being traded in for every new, at-the-money option.

OTHER OPTION TRICKS

There are a few other ways to alter how options function as an incentive, a retention tool, and as a means to accumulate long-term wealth. Specifically:

- Shorten the option term. Virtually all options granted today have a 10-year term. More and more companies, however, are talking about or implementing shorter terms, such as three to five years. Shorter terms reduce the value—and accounting cost—of the options, but because they expire much sooner, they also limit the potential problems caused by underwater options. After these options are retired, new options can be issued in their place (without the hassle and the expense of a repricing).

- Post-termination vesting. To give retiring CEOs and other top executives an incentive to leave the company in excellent condition, they can be granted options that do not vest until three to five years after their retirement or other termination (not for cause).

- Discounted options. Perhaps my favorite option trick, this little-used technique gives executives an option with an exercise price that is significantly less than the current market price. Discounted options can be an excellent deferral device. Let's say that an executive has $50,000 in bonus that he or she would like to defer, i.e., not be taxed on currently. Instead of receiving the $50,000 in cash, the executive can receive 10,000 options at a $10 exercise price when the stock is trading at $15. (So if exercised today, he or she would have a $50,000 gain.) This allows the executive to recognize the deferred income whenever he or she wants to just by exercising the option. This provides far more flexibility than with most standard deferral programs. The executive, of course, is taking some risk the stock price may go down. It is very similar to deferring the bonus and investing in company stock—with the added flexibility of having access to it whenever you want it. An exciting variation on discounted options is performance-vesting discounted options, where the executive earns the right to exercise the option based on achieving individual, division, or company performance goals.

- Required holding period. To mitigate situations where executives exercise their options and immediately sell the stock, a required holding period can be implemented. When an option is exercised, the executive must hold the stock acquired for at least one to two years. This is a very effective way to make options a longer-term incentive. However requiring 100 percent of the stock to be held on 100 percent of the options may make it overly difficult for some employees to exercise these options. Consequently it may be more effective to have a required holding period on a percentage of the options. Then the rest of the shares can be sold to cover the taxes and the cash required to exercise the options. This last option trick, required holding period, is gaining favor quickly. Several companies have implemented this feature. Investor groups and watchdog groups are heralding this feature as a simple solution to the otherwise short-term orientation of executive options.

The coming reality of an expense for options should lead companies to ask deeper philosophical questions about their compensation policies—specifically whether or not to use options and, if so, how they should be structured. To make that decision companies must define the purpose for the option plan and how it fits in with the overall compensation philosophy and desired risk orientation of the firm.

WHAT DO YOU THINK?

- Assuming your company has stock options, what purposes do they serve and what objectives are achieved by having them in the compensation structure?

- Given that the new accounting rules will make it easier to use more performance-based options, what form of options would be most effective for achieving your company's objectives? Is there a better mix of options and other incentives (restricted stock, performance-vested restricted stock, stock ownership, etc.) that would be more directly supportive of your company's objectives, and more cost effective?

BRINGING BALANCE TO EXECUTIVE COMPENSATION

We've looked at making options more performance based. This is an important part of creating a more sane and balanced executive compensation system.

Graef "Bud" Crystal has been called the leading expert on executive compensation in America. Now a full-time columnist for Bloomberg News, Crystal is an eloquent and outspoken critic of excessive executive pay. He has written hundreds of articles on the subject as well as several books, including *In Search of Excess: The Overcompensation of American Executives* and *What Are You Worth?: Playing the Pay Game Fairly*. The former editor of the CrystalReport.com online newsletter, Crystal has testified on Capitol Hill and has served as a consultant to the Securities and Exchange Commission (SEC) and the Financial Accounting Standards Board (FASB). For years he was an adjunct professor of industrial relations and organizational behavior at the Haas School of Business at University of California at Berkeley. Before beginning this second career as executive pay critic, Crystal headed the executive compensation practice at Towers Perrin. Crystal and I discussed our views on executive compensation, stock options grants, and a vision for the future.

Delves: I am inspired by the work that you've done, particularly what you've written about the state of executive compensation today. What is your vision for the future? If executive compensation evolved into something more accountable and efficient, what would it look like?

Crystal: To me the linchpin of getting any change is a charge to earnings for options. This whole area is out of control.

Delves: Yes. To me the issue is not whether to value options, but how to value them. There continues to be a lot of debate over how options should be valued, including the methodology used. Clearly there is as much art to this as science.

Crystal: I remember in the last round in 1993 [when the FASB attempted to require stock-option expensing]. I remember one of the members of the board saying to me, "What do you say to the fact that Black-Scholes is not totally precise, that people can't agree to the last penny on what it should be." I told him, "If you think it's hard to value an option, try estimating the present value of retiree medical costs for procedures that haven't been invented yet. Even the decision of how many years to depreciate an asset. It's a straw man. Of course it's imprecise. So is much of everything else."

Delves: My position is just because it's difficult doesn't mean we shouldn't do it. We've tackled far harder things as a society than option valuation.

Crystal: The first thing is to have some reasonable charge for options. Then, I think, companies are going to stop granting them in such huge doses. You have to understand, pay is log-normally distributed, such that the average is always higher than the median. When you start talking about stock options grants, they are so log-normally distributed that you can drive 16 semis abreast between the median and the average, and there would still be room for a few more. That's because of the mega grants. When the froth goes out of that with the charge to earnings for options, companies are going to say, "We can't afford it any more. We are going to have to cut back." Then the average is going to start dropping closer to the median. So in essence the typical CEO may not see his pay cut so much. But the [compensation for top executives such as] Michael Eisner, the 40-million share grant to Larry Ellison, and the 20-million-share grant to Steve Jobs, that's going to come off. If not an outright decrease, then at least a slowing of an increase.

Delves: What doesn't make sense, if you think about it, is the dramatic rise in executive compensation compared with the actual market for executive talent.

Crystal: Any time that you see the pay of a given occupation rising at a disproportionate rate to other occupations, then you're seeing either an excess of demand for people in that occupation, shrinkage of supply, or sometimes both. Now look at CEOs. Their pay has gone up wildly compared with other occupations. Has there been a decrease in supply? No. Business schools have been turning them out by the hundreds for years. It's also hard to argue that there's a decrease in supply when there are quite a few talented women and minorities who are totally denied an opportunity. Then someone might say there must be an increase in demand. Not exactly. For every company that is split in two or three pieces, there are many more that combine and merge. There is no rationality for the way these people are paid. The main reason why there is no correlation between pay and performance is because the losers won't take their lumps. They say the fact that they've underperformed shows that they need more motivation!

Delves: It appears that there's a hole in the market for CEO talent. In other professions, pay goes up and down. When it comes to CEOs, compensation does not seem to respond to market forces. It just goes up.

Crystal: In order to have a market, you need an informed buyer and an informed seller, plus vigorous arms-length negotiations. We've got an informed seller. But boards don't spend much time on this. They don't have independent advice. And mainly the boards are made of up CEOs of other companies who don't have any philo-sophical distaste for higher pay. They love it.

Delves: As I've started to go through this exercise in light of the expected expensing for stock options, I've noticed that the attitude of some companies is, "That's awfully complex. Isn't there an easier way to do an incentive plan?" My response is, "Yes! Let's set some financial goals two or three years out and build an incentive plan around that. Let's forget about stock price, but look instead at the drivers of value."

Crystal: I haven't seen any evidence that options motivate anything. It's amazing. Let's say you went to a doctor because you were feeling ill and he gave you a shot, then the next day you were sick as a dog and near death. If you went back to that doctor and he said, "Well, now I'm going to give you an even bigger shot of the same medicine," I think you would change doctors.

CHAPTER EIGHT

Designing a Balanced Portfolio of Incentives

Risk and reward are two essential elements that, when in balance, result in effective executive compensation. When a portion of compensation is at risk—meaning it must be earned through the attainment of certain goals and performance targets—executives should have an incentive to take bolder, more decisive actions. The rewards for taking these risks and succeeding include salary, incentives, promotion opportunities, recognition, prestige, and more.

The real challenge for companies, however, is not how to get people to take risks but how to get them to take the *right risks* by offering them the *right incentives*. More directly, how does a company get its managers to take risks with the company's money that are in the best interests of the company, its shareholders, and other constituents? How does the company create an environment in which executives are motivated to take personal risks congruent with the kinds of risks the company should be taking? The answers to these questions are at the core of effective compensation and incentive design.

THE RISK DECISION

When designing executive pay programs, there is a lot of discussion about aligning executive and shareholder interests. The goal is to have executives take risks and make decisions shareholders would want. Shareholders, after all, invest in a company's stock expecting a certain level of return in exchange for a certain level of risk. This risk/return trade-off is slightly different for every company and every stock. Ideally executives would make decisions and take actions producing the exact combination of company risk and stock return that shareholders expect. But first companies must understand the difference between an executive's risk and return and the company's risk and return. A good incentive program bridges that gap and makes those risk/return scenarios as close as possible.

Stock options carry a combination of risk and return that is almost certainly not the right combination for every company. They are usually too blunt a tool used to encourage forward thinking and entrepreneurial behavior. Let's say Executive A is given $10,000 to "invest" at the gaming tables in Las Vegas. He is told he may keep 10 percent of all winnings, but there will be no consequence or responsibility for any losses. That would produce one set of "investments" (or bets). On the other hand Executive B is sent to the gaming tables with $10,000 and told she may keep 10 percent of the winnings but must also pay 10 percent of any losses out of her own pocket. Clearly that would produce a different risk orientation and most likely result in a different set of actions—at least in theory.

Stock options produce the risk orientation and behavior of Executive A. Outright stock ownership is closer to the scenario of Executive B. The lesson here is that different incentives create different risk orientation and behavior. Thus they have to be considered based on what kinds of risks a company wants its executives to take with its money. To do that companies must understand the psychology of risk and how it affects behavior.

THE PSYCHOLOGY OF RISK

Most people are by nature risk averse. Given the choice most people would go for the "sure thing" rather than risk everything on a long shot. In order for people to take on greater risk, they must see the potential for a greater reward, especially if it can be earned through some means within their control. This is particularly true of executives and other corporate employees who want the regularity and reliability of a paycheck, health care benefits, a pension plan, and the potential for a long-term career.

The typical corporate executive differs in this regard from certain other professionals who not only have a high tolerance for risk but also embrace it. Commodity and stock traders make their living—and potentially a very good one—by facing enormous risks. It's not uncommon for a professional trader to have six-figure swings in profit and loss from day to day. By nature these people are far less risk-averse than the average person. But they are only willing to take on that enormous risk because there is the potential for a substantial reward.

Companies also have their own risk profile, given the type of business they engage in, their corporate culture, and so forth. A public utility, for example, has a far different risk profile than an Internet company. A company's risk profile can also change—and sometimes very rapidly. This may be in response to a management change, a shift in strategic direction, or a change in the regulatory environment. Consider the savings and loan (S&L) institutions of the 1980s. Within 18 months following deregulation, they went from investing primarily in housing to investing heavily in junk bonds. This sparked a crisis in which the government had to intervene at an immense cost. Somewhere along the line, management and the boards of those S&Ls did not adequately deal with the change in the risk profile of their organizations. In more recent history Enron used to be a conservative pipeline company until it transformed itself into an ultra-high-risk energy trading company.

A compensation program, therefore, must address each of these elements of risk: executives' risk tolerance, the company's risk profile, and shareholders' expectation for the kinds of risks the company and its executives will take on.

FROM BUREAUCRATS TO INNOVATIVE THINKERS

Risks are a necessary part of business. Taking on healthy risks— such as innovative thinking, developing new products, opening a new market, trying new ways of doing things—moves a company forward. Embracing these kinds of risks can make a company more competitive and more profitable.

Getting executives to take risks, however, has traditionally been a difficult thing. In the 1970s and early 1980s, executives tended to act more like bureaucrats, who sought to preserve the status quo. This seemed to be the name of the game. Then, as outlined in Chapter 2, LBOs and MBOs introduced a new breed of empowered executive who willingly made bold decisions. The reason was simple: these executives acted more like owners because they took on significant personal risk, given the amount of wealth they had on the line. In the principal-agent relationship that defines most public companies and their executives, this new breed of corporate leaders crossed the line. They were both agent and principal. As a result, they made decisions with far greater boldness and expediency.

Traditional companies tried to replicate this behavior with stock ownership and then stock options. This approach, however, fell short of the mark. Now the challenge for companies and their boards is to offer incentives that encourage executives and employees to take risks in the best interests of the company. Positive, healthy risk-taking encourages people to try new approaches, become more innovative, and otherwise "think outside the box" of routine behavior.

Increasingly companies want more innovation and creativity from their employees. In the age of human capital and information, companies are beginning to value the contribution of the individual even more than the contribution of traditional capital. To make the most of that human capital, people need to think independently, make decisions, and take actions that have some level of risk associated with them.

TAKING A HEALTHY RISK

There are many examples of the encouragement of healthy risk. Over the past 20 to 30 years, more and more factories have been instituting gain-sharing and other group incentive plans to encourage more innovative thinking among workers to benefit the company and increase productivity. For employees to do this requires some risk in the form of pointing out problems, disagreeing with the status quo, offering constructive criticism, and trying new things. These are all risky behaviors most factory workers would not have considered earlier. But with the potential reward of gain-sharing or other incentives, these workers have eagerly risen to the challenge.

Understanding this risk-reward correlation, companies can encourage executive or employee performance by putting at least part of their compensation at risk. This is where bonuses and incentives come in. An example of this is in the City of Chicago, which routinely puts incentives into its large public works contracts, such as for the rebuilding of an expressway. If the contractor finishes early, the payment is more. If the contractor finishes late, payment is less. The contractor has greater risk but can also reap greater rewards for better performance.

A classic case of compensation risk-reward is the 100 percent commission salesperson. With all of their pay based upon commission, these sales people live by their own efforts. If they don't sell, they don't make anything. On the other hand, they also have significantly more upside and potential reward than other people at their career level. That's why top salespeople sometimes make more than senior executives. Despite that potential reward, the risks may be more than some people can handle, which is why not everybody goes into sales.

Drawing on these two examples, however, it's clear that when at least a portion of compensation is at risk, then it can become a powerful incentive for innovative thinking, decision-making, and action. This is not always the case with stock options, which provide plenty of potential reward but very little risk.

With stock options, if the stock goes up for whatever reason, then the options pay off. If the stock does not go up, then the option does not pay off. Period. That's the extent of the downside for the executive, who does not have to risk one dime of his or her own capital in order to receive the options. Stock options only directly reward stock price increases—nothing else. In addition the vast majority of stock option grants do not have any stipulations on the rise in stock price. They don't specify when the stock should rise, how far it should rise, or how long it should be sustained at a higher level. Nor do these grants specify what types of risks should be taken to accelerate the stock performance.

Because the amount of option grants typically overshadows all other forms of compensation, stock options significantly impact the risk profile of the executive. Too many options also change the risk profile of the company. In turn this may result in a level of risk at the company that exceeds shareholder expectations. We are living with the legacy of the huge number of stock options that have been granted, which has vastly increased the potential for unhealthy risk.

Without any stipulation, the underlying—if unspoken—message of large option grants was to get the stock price up at virtually any cost and with any risk. Fortunately the majority of company executives did not take the bait of unhealthy risk. But enough did, as evidenced by the corporate scandals of 2001 and 2002, which underscore the problem.

It is interesting to note, however, that the average volatility of stock prices has dramatically increased since the mid-1990s. The historic volatility of the S&P 500 has grown steadily from a low of 5 percent in September 1995 to nearly 22 percent at the end of 2002. While there are many factors contributing to this increased volatility, we have to acknowledge the fact that stock options had something to do with this. Loading executives of virtually all large publicly traded companies with stock options may have had some dramatic impact on the market as a whole. These executives had a significant incentive to make their stock more volatile, and hence more risky, because of their stock options. Options on a more volatile stock are worth more than options on a less volatile stock. Hence the stock option epidemic of the last 10 years may have served to significantly destabilize and increase the risk level of our capital markets. Perhaps this is why Fed Chairman Alan Greenspan has been so concerned about this issue.

When it comes to future compensation packages, companies take the perspective of the end goal. What are the specific performance targets, behaviors, and risks the company wants to encourage? With that in mind, are options the correct incentive? Do executives already hold so many unexercised options that these incentives continue to be a primary driver of their behavior? Does the company like the type of behavior among its senior executives and other employees that the risk/reward scenario cultivates?

THE BALANCED PORTFOLIO APPROACH

Clearly options need to be balanced going forward with other forms of incentives and have features to make them more performance-based. Just as a diversified portfolio of investments allows an individual to reap rewards under an array of circumstances and market conditions, a balanced portfolio of incentives creates the same type of diversification. For the entire portfolio of incentives to pay off, the company would have to reach its targets in all areas. If targets were hit in some areas but missed in others, then certain components of the incentive portfolio would pay off while others would pay off less or not at all.

In order to establish a balanced portfolio of incentives, companies must draw a direct connection between incentives and specific performance measures. When a measure is selected, a goal or target is determined. Then the company must decide how much risk is acceptable and appropriate for achieving this goal.

The amount of risk that an executive faces can be influenced in three ways:

1. The percentage of total pay at risk through incentives.
2. The amount of potential reward allocated to each particular performance measure.
3. The amount of leverage (the trade-off between change in pay and change in performance) applied to the incentive formula (addressed later in this chapter).

The incentive rewards offered for taking these risks will also vary from company to company. The incentive may be paid in cash, stock, restricted stock, etc. Stock options may be part of the mix.

A balanced portfolio of incentives serves two important purposes. First, it helps to ensure excellent short-term and long-term financial performance. It also underscores the fundamentals of a solid, healthy business.

The incentive portfolio should send a strong message to executives that their job is to maintain and build a solid, healthy business that produces strong and consistent financial returns to its owners. (The stock price, however, should not be the main consideration, and may not even be a primary focus but rather the result of good management and good results.) The company's goals should not end here.

For a truly balanced approach, however, companies cannot consider only financial performance targets. A company should also have satisfied customers, a robust market share, innovative and necessary products and services, and motivated employees who are growing and developing within the organization. A company should strive to be a responsible member of the community and a steward of the environment. These are the reasons why a corporation exists, not just to generate a higher stock price.

Are these goals difficult to define, target, and measure? Yes, though that should not be a deterrent. After all, executives are responsible for doing all these things—it's part of their job. Their performance in each of these areas should be gauged, and their pay should be impacted accordingly.

Only a solid, financially sound company can develop its people, contribute responsibly to the community, and maintain the environment. These actions put the emphasis on the long-term well-being of the company instead of short-term stock performance. When the company focuses on the long term, it sends a powerful message to its executives that they, too, must take a long-term view. This will influence their behavior, decisions, and actions.

More importantly a company must resist being held captive to the vicissitudes of stock analysts every quarter. Stock analysts are not investors, and neither are portfolio managers. They are managers for investors, many of whom also tend to have a short-term focus. Despite this short-term focus, companies and their boards should reexamine their obligation to shareholders. It is not just to increase short-term stock performance but rather to create sustainable growth and value through responsible, innovative management over the next 5, 10, or 20 years.

Promoting a longer-term view, Coca-Cola announced in December 2002 that beginning in 2003 it would no longer provide quarterly or annual earnings "guidance" to analysts. Instead the soft-drink company said it would comment on and provide perspective for its "value drivers, its strategic initiatives, and those factors critical to understanding its business and operating environment." Since this bold move, many other companies have followed suit.

Another important component in the balanced portfolio is that good performance has to be rewarded—and rewarded well. If companies want their executives to perform, they must pay them and pay them well. Just because a company adopts performance measures or expects certain risks to be taken in return for rewards doesn't mean it has to skimp on compensation. On the contrary, these performance measures and incentives should be a means to reward excellence with potentially lucrative payouts, bonuses, and other compensation.

Components of the Balanced Incentive Portfolio

How, then, can a company establish a balanced incentive portfolio? The best approach is to use a performance matrix like the one shown below in Figure 8-1. Across the top are short-term, medium-term, and long-term time frames. Listed along the side are a variety of possible criteria.

Using this matrix companies can determine their top priorities for the short term, medium term, and long term. While each of the criteria is important, not all of them can be targeted for each time frame. Certain criteria must be selected and highlighted for each time frame. To identify priorities, ask the following questions:

- Which criteria have the highest priority?
- Which ones have the greatest potential for improvement?

FIGURE 8-1

Performance Matrix

Indicate relative importance of each measure by placing "Low, Medium, or High" in the related box

Performance Measures	Short Term	Medium Term	Long Term
Earnings Performance			
Return (on Assets, Investment, Equity, etc.			
Stock Performance Measures			
Marketing Performance Measures			
Employee Satisfaction/ Development			
Community Citizenship			
Environmental Stewardship			

- Which ones have the greatest impact on the bottom line, shareholder value, etc.?
- Which ones do not have a short-term impact on the bottom line but are essential for the future of the company?
- Which measures may be negatively impacted in the short run as a trade-off for higher performance in the long run?
- Which ones are the company willing to pay for and willing to pay the most for?

By answering these questions, patterns and overlaps will emerge. The result will identify the top priorities for the company on a short-term, medium-term, and long-term basis. Let's say, for example, that under the "earnings" heading, a company identifies short-term profit growth and long-term margin improvement; both are assigned a high priority. Under "return," the measure is return on equity (ROE) as a long-term objective and also a high priority. Stock performance is a long-term goal but it's a medium priority. Market share is both a short-term goal and a high priority. Employee satisfaction and community/environmental stewardship are all medium- to long-term goals but are assigned a low priority.

The end result of this exercise may be to design an annual incentive plan that focuses on earnings growth and market share and a long-term incentive plan that targets margin and ROE, with a secondary emphasis on stock performance and a small component for employee satisfaction and community responsibility.

After company-wide targets and priorities have been established, the next question is which people, functions, and jobs in the company are the most responsible for executing each aspect of the performance matrix. In many companies incentive plans will vary from job to job simply because of what is within or beyond a person's job description and realm of influence. Thus the incentive plan for the vice president of sales may be different from the plan for the vice president of human resources.

Looking at this hypothetical set of corporate priorities, would stock options be part of the compensation plan? Maybe or maybe not. What's clear, however, is that the company would want to offer some equity-based incentives (stock, options, or a combination) that are earned based on margin and ROE improvements over a two- to four-year period. Once the targets are identified and the priorities set, the types of incentives offering the appropriate risk and potential rewards automatically follow.

Using Leverage

One tool to use in the balanced portfolio of incentives is leverage. In this context leverage reflects how much compensation can go up and down as well as how easily it can go up and down. With leverage a company can offer the highest payout for the highest performance, a minimal payout for standard performance, and no payout for anything falling below a threshold level of performance.

For example a company sets a goal to increase its profit margin from 15 percent to 20 percent, with a promise of a $50,000 bonus if the target is met. In a low-leverage incentive plan, if the 15 percent margin is maintained, the executive receives a $40,000 bonus. At 16 percent, the bonus rises to $42,000; at 17 percent, $44,000; and so on up to 20 percent, at which point the bonus is $50,000. If the margin exceeds the target and rises to 25 percent, then the bonus is $60,000. Under this low-leverage plan (see Figure 8-2), if the margin shows

FIGURE 8-2

High- and Low-Leverage Incentive Plans

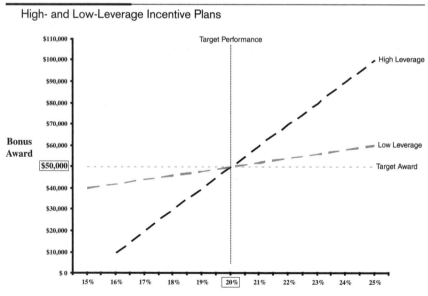

Profit Margin

any increase but falls short of the target, there is still a sizeable bonus. The relative difference between getting the margin to 18 percent and hitting the 20 percent target is not all that great.

Under a high-leverage incentive plan, if the margin rises from 15 to 16 percent, the payout is $10,000. But below 16 percent, the payout is zero. Conversely for every percentage-point increase in margin above 16 percent, the incentive rises by $10,000, paying out the full $50,000 at 20 percent and escalating even more dramatically as the target is exceeded. By the time margins reach 22 percent, the bonus escalates to $100,000.

The size of the reward and the amount of leverage used should correlate directly with the amount of risk executives take—as well as the investment in time, talent, and effort necessary to reach the goal. The amount of risk companies introduce into the equation also depends upon several factors, including the potential for improvement and the value of that improvement. For example if a company were starting a new production line that was barely profitable but had the potential of expanding margins quickly, then a steep-slope, high-leverage incentive plan would be appropriate. But if, realistically, a company could only expect incremental increases in margin (or another performance measure), then a low-leverage plan would be more appropriate.

THE BENEFIT OF STOCK OWNERSHIP

Over the years I've seen some positive results from stock ownership required by executives. Stock ownership provides a clear illustration of what happens when you put people directly at risk. It may not work for all companies, but for many firms, it has worked very well.

One such example is health-care company Baxter International, which requires executives and some managers to own a certain amount of stock. Similar stock-ownership requirements were adopted by Allegiance, a Baxter spin-off later acquired by Cardinal Health. At Baxter stock ownership was largely mandatory, while at Allegiance it was voluntary. In order to fund the stock purchases, executives borrowed a significant amount of money to buy the stock. A vice president making $200,000 to $300,000 a year, for example, might have to borrow some $200,000 to purchase stock. The most senior people in the company had to invest about $1 million in stock.

The stock-purchase loans were very carefully structured so that dividends were sufficient to pay the interest on the loans. However these were full-recourse, third-party loans with no guarantee from the company (although Baxter did offer some limited downside protection).

What happened after the stock ownership plan was instituted was extraordinary. Baxter's stock had been a lackluster performer for about 10 years. When executives were required to acquire and hold significant amounts of company stock, however, they began thinking and acting differently. Their heads were more in the game because their wallets were on the line. The company began operating significantly better, and the stock price advanced—to the benefit of all shareholders. Replicating the stock ownership plan of its former parent, Allegiance did especially well in the period it was an independent company, with its stock going up fivefold over that time.

This illustrates the fact that real ownership with real money at stake can make a difference in executive motivation and behavior. Stock ownership introduces a kind of healthy, long-term risk that holds the potential for capital accumulation tied to the success of the company.

A REVOLUTIONARY STOCK CONCEPT

The shine has faded on stock options. Companies are questioning their universal usefulness and reassessing the propriety of granting vast amounts of options to virtually every executive. Nonetheless, as we rethink the use of stock options, it is important that we don't lose sight of the underlying concept: the movement to share company ownership on a large scale still has merit.

In the heat of our love affair with the "new economy" in the mid- to late-1990s, we started to believe that the rules of business had changed. We saw that human beings and information would replace both physical and financial capital as the backbone of commerce. This was and is absolutely true (as discussed further in Chapter 9). We have entered into a new era, and our compensation system needs to reflect that.

It's true that I consider stock options a largely failed experiment in that direction, principally because options are an ineffective instrument with too many drawbacks. However this should not stop us in our quest to value human capital and to share the benefits and responsibilities of ownership with a broad base of employees.

Corporate America has not even begun to tap the potential uses of other financial instruments, including various forms of stock and ownership we have yet to devise. I believe it is completely possible to develop classes of stock or other instruments that allow employees to earn and reap the benefits of ownership over time and recognize that employees have become *the* critical component in the economic process of an organization. I challenge all of us to use our critical knowledge and wisdom to truly think outside the box and develop new forms and types of ownership reflecting the growing value of human capital.

WHAT DO YOU THINK?

- What is your company's risk-orientation?
  Would you consider your company to be, for example, ultra-conservative, cautiously progressive, strategically aggressive, innovative and edgy, or a total maverick?
- How is your company's risk profile reflected in and reinforced by its compensation programs?
  Conversely in what ways is your compensation system at odds with your company's desired risk profile?
- Do stock options create the proper risk orientation for your company and culture?
- What mix of incentives and stock ownership would be most effective and desirable at your company?

BUILDING A BALANCED INCENTIVE PROGRAM

BorgWarner Inc., a New York Stock Exchange-traded automotive supplier, has two compensation and incentive programs driving the company's performance. Its annual Management Incentive Plan (MIP) is based on economic value added (EVA). While this plan pays out annually, it is based on performance over three years. It also uses an Executive Stock Plan (ESP), which awards stock to senior executives based on the company's performance relative to its peers. While BorgWarner does grant stock options, these are not a major feature of its plans. Under recently retired Chairman and CEO John Fiedler, BorgWarner was a consistently strong performer in a cyclical and highly competitive industry. Over the last five years, BorgWarner has emerged as the acknowledged leader in the OEM (original equipment manufacturer) market. John Fiedler and I discussed BorgWarner's view of incentives and executive compensation.

Delves: BorgWarner's incentive program is a very well thought out plan. What led you to the decision to de-emphasize stock options and emphasize the long-term stock-ownership plan?

Fiedler: What led us to that decision is that we're in a cyclical business. With options, in a cyclical business, people get rewarded for reasons they had no control over. And they get punished for reasons that they had no control over. Further when options were worth a lot of money, it did not correlate with what people's efforts had been. And when options were down, it also didn't correlate with what people's efforts had been.

We came up with things to replace it. Our Management Incentive Plan (MIP) goes very, very deep into the organization—right down to the plant manager and his staff. Our Executive Stock Plan (ESP) is also very important. In the ESP, instead of granting options, we award stock to senior executives. Not only do we award stock to the person, but we also award cash to pay the taxes so that they can afford to hold the stock. That's why it has been limited and probably always will be limited to the top 15 people in the company. You just can't afford to go any lower.

Delves: Do you use stock options at all?

Fiedler: We do use stock options for middle management and for other uses at the very top of the house but really very lightly. Probably we will not use them as accounting standards change.

Delves: Tell me more about the MIP and how it works.

Fiedler: MIP is really a modified EVA (economic value added) program. Pure EVA does not work in our business. Our program, importantly, covers a three-year period and not just a one-year period. The program also pays people for improvement in EVA. Thus it's a delta EVA program.

Let's say a division has a positive EVA of $110 million while another division has a negative EVA of $78 million. But guess what? If you're in the poor-performing division and you get your EVA from negative $78 million to negative $73 million, you make more money than the person in the better-performing division who gets EVA from positive $110 million to $112 million.

Delves: Interestingly, the MIP program has a three-year life, instead of just a one-year target.

Fiedler: Yes, that allows people to make long-term investments in their businesses without being penalized. For example if a division wants to invest $10 million, it is charged for $5 million in capital the first year, and then (an additional) $2.5 million the second year and $2.5 million the following year. You know what you're going to be charged, and you know your cash flow. Also because of the cyclical nature of our industry, the three-year program includes what I think is the most masterful thing. We have what we call the "look-back."

Let's say that you have a bad year and don't make what you're supposed to make. So if you were the CEO, you could have made a $500,000 bonus [but] instead you only made $200,000. The reason you didn't make it was the industry was in a downturn. I don't care how hard you work; there is no way you're going to make those goals. So do we give you a special exception? Do we go to the board and cry? We say, no way. That $300,000 doesn't go away; it doesn't evaporate. You have a chance to earn at least part of it back in the future.

Delves: So if someone misses out on a bonus in one year, they have the next year to make it up.

Fiedler: Exactly. And our people see this as fair. Not only that but they tend to say, "I didn't get it this year—but wait 'til you see next year!'"

Delves: Do you see any drawbacks to the three-year MIP plan?

Fiedler: There is one thing. We just hired a new senior executive. But it will take us three years to get him into the MIP program. We're loath to go back and reward him for the past when he wasn't here. On the other hand he wouldn't get the first payout for three years. So we are bridging that gap with stock options. We talked it over with the board. The board said, "We don't care if we have to expense them. We're not going to give that up as a transition." That being said an executive coming into the company would rather be part of MIP because stock options are still stock options. They still are going to get rewarded at the wrong times and punished at the wrong times.

Delves: Let's talk for a minute about the ESP program. This program for senior executives has an important competitive component.

Fiedler: We have a peer group. This year there are 16 companies in it. Now for the next three years—from 2003 through the end of 2005— we'll see how well we do versus that peer group. We're going to reward people stock and cash to pay the taxes on the stock based on that. The program kicks in around 40 percent, and 100 percent is the maximum bonus. It's skewed toward the top end.

Delves: As part of the ESP, I understand that your top executives are required to own significant amounts of shares.

Fiedler: I have to hold three years of total compensation as stock. We've worked it up from salary to cash compensation and then to total compensation. Executive vice presidents have to hold two years, and vice presidents have to hold one year.

    To add another wrinkle to it, all of a sudden one of our executive vice presidents came to me and said, "I'm holding more Borg-Warner stock than I'm required to. I should really sell some for the good of my family." I said to him, "I don't want you to sell it. How can I give you an incentive to keep it?" So we got together with the board. We have a program now that for all the stock he has beyond what he was required to have, we give him an option for more stock.

Delves: Clearly the centerpiece of corporate incentive and rewards at BorgWarner is the MIP.

Fiedler: We are getting very specific results and very measurable results from it. We're doing a lot better as result of the compensation program. Specifically we've been measuring our return on assets and return on investment. We set specific targets that we knew we needed to achieve in order to beat our competition. And that's partly how we backed into our goals for the MIP program. As we hit those goals, we are achieving those rates of return on investments that we need to beat the competition, and to improve our stock performance.

Delves: The overall reaction to MIP has been positive among your executive team. That proves that the rewards offered are lucrative enough to motivate your executives to take the appropriate risks and actions to improve performance.

Fiedler: This has worked very, very well for us. Let me give you an example. A couple of years ago we bought a German turbocharger company. We had a lot of people telling me that the Germans don't understand this type of capitalism, they have a different work ethic, etc. They like to employ lots of people and they are happy to spend $1.20 for $1.00 worth of revenue. Well we put them on the same MIP plan as everyone else in the company, and we educated them on how it worked. They were skeptical about it at first, but they did very well by it the first year. I went over there and delivered the checks to everybody. All of a sudden, they became believers. They became highly focused on the numbers and hitting the goals. And they made very good money off this program. They have made dramatic changes to how they run their business. Now I'm not sure if they believe in our way of doing things in their hearts. But they sure do in their actions. There is no way I could have integrated that organization into the company without this incentive program.

CHAPTER NINE

Building Healthy Employee-Employer Contracts for Public and Private Companies

Stock options are more than just a compensation issue. Over the past decade stock options, particularly in large quantities, have played a huge part in the set of agreements between the employee and employer that is often referred to as a contract. In many cases these contracts—whether written or implied—were skewed by stock options with their promise of potentially large and lucrative rewards.

Certainly stock options were *de rigueur* at Internet and other high-tech start-ups, often in lieu of cash compensation. The tacit agreement for employees in return for working hard was to receive options that some day, maybe, could pay off big. The reality in these situations was the companies granted stock options because they didn't have sufficient cash to pay people—and everybody knew that. In other words if you went to work at a start-up, you knew what you were getting into and you knew the options you received were a big gamble that may or may not pay off.

I can remember in the 1980s, a college friend went to work for a Silicon Valley technology company and another friend went to work for a software company. Both received a lot of stock and options, and both were paid less cash. They understood there was a possibility, although not a probability, that these options could pay off very well in five or seven years—or not. As young 20-something executives in those days, it was a worthwhile experience to be part of a start-up and to invest some sweat equity in return for a possible payoff. If things turned out, they'd be laughing all the way to the bank. If not, then they gained valuable experience.

The other healthy element in these kinds of arrangements was that the people going to work for the technology start-ups were fairly risk-tolerant. They were interested in working for that kind of company and taking the kind of risks that go with it. More traditional-minded people preferred to work for an established company with a regular paycheck and a competitive wage.

The practice of granting stock options to employees was not limited to technology start-ups. Well-established firms such as Microsoft, Intel, and Cisco continue to have broad-based plans under which options are granted through the employee ranks. These plans, in fact, have been one of the most pronounced results of the technology boom. While executives usually still receive the lion's share of the options, huge numbers of options (at least in the aggregate) are also granted to employees. Part of the rationale for these technology companies was a "share the wealth" mentality that recognized the importance of human capital in their business equation.

While the "share the wealth" philosophy in stock options is associated with technology companies, it did not start there. In the mid-1980s Pepsico became the first large company to grant options to all employees under what is still called its "Share Power" plan. The plan was instituted to offer employees long-term capital accumulation and a chance to share in the long-term growth of the company. In fact it was—and still is—communicated as a program that will help employees accumulate wealth over 10 to 15 years. At the time Pepsico instituted the program, it was a bold and unprecedented move, shocking the compensation world by granting options to more than 100,000 employees.

In my mind Pepsico's "Share Power" plan is part of a healthy contract between employer and employee for two important reasons. First of all it focuses on the long term, encouraging employees to wait 5, 10, or 15 years in order for the plan to really pay off. Second the plan provides additional savings and capital accumulation for the employee's future, especially retirement. The "Share Power" plan was not sold to employees in any other way.

AN UNHEALTHY CONTRACT

Stock options turned sour, however, in the age of "irrational exuberance" when, in the mid- to late-1990s, it looked like there was only up and no down in the stock market. Against this backdrop the stock option went from being a means of sharing in the corporate long-term pie to a get-rich-quick scheme. Add to that our false expectations about the "new economy," which led us to believe that the old rules of business did not apply. Technology was king, and we touted everything "virtual"—even virtual earnings. Technology and Internet companies were going public with little more than a concept and a business plan, and sometimes seeing their stocks double, triple, quadruple, and more.

In this type of business environment, stock options added to the irrationality of our exuberance. Moreover they negatively impacted the explicit and implicit contracts that were the underpinning of employment. Anytime someone goes to work for a company, there is at least an understanding, if not an actual contract, that for a specific job and specific set of expectations, a person will be paid a certain amount. Other elements of the contract usually involve loyalty in exchange for longevity. The employee receives growth and development opportunities in exchange for innovation and putting forth the required extra effort. Promotions, raises, and bonuses go hand in hand with strong performance.

When stock options entered into the mix, the contract became false, undeliverable, and impossible to execute. The reason? Unlike a start-up, in which employees and management understood and recognized the gamble, people began to see the stock options as a "sure thing." Now the implied agreement was to work long hours and sacrifice your personal life and in two or three years—possibly sooner—you *will* be able to make a large amount of money.

Tales abound of mid-level John and Jane Does who made anywhere from half-a-million to several million dollars from stock options. It wasn't hard to find a 20-something millionaire in the 1990s. There was a common expression at technology companies for people who had lots of options worth so much they had no incentive to work anymore: "Let them vest in peace." The only reason they stayed was because another few million in option value had not vested. This became part of the modern myth to which everyone aspired. They felt they were being cheated if they didn't share in it.

What few people saw or were willing to admit at the time was these were false promises born out of an overinflated stock market and unrealistic expectations for future growth—along with large stock option grants. The contracts between employer and employee became narrow, limited, and unhealthy (see Figure 9-1).

One of the classic cases of a bad contract at the CEO level was George Shaheen and Webvan. In 1999 Shaheen was the managing partner of what was then Andersen Consulting (now Accenture), where he had earned a reputation as a skilled and successful leader. According to press reports, during his tenure revenues increased to $8.3 billion from $1.1 billion.

Shaheen's departure in October of that year to become CEO of Webvan, an online grocery retailer, was shocking. Why would he want to leave a prestigious job where he earned a reported $4 million a year for an Internet start-up with no profits? The answer is easy when you consider his employment agreement with Webvan: Shaheen was paid $500,000, received an outright grant of 1,250,000 shares of Webvan stock worth $10 million at the time, and received options on another *15 million shares of stock* with a market exercise price of $8 per share. In other words he received options on $120 million in stock. For every $1 increase in the stock price, he would have made $15 million.

FIGURE 9-1

Healthy versus Unhealthy Employee Contracts

Healthy	Unhealthy
Work hard, be part of corporate culture, have healthy and balanced lifestyle, grow with the company.	Work hard, sacrifice personal life.
In return, receive salary, bonus, long-term incentives, training, feedback, good people to work with, and challenging work.	In return get rich in 2 to 3 years or sooner.

Shaheen, however, resigned 18 months later in the wake of Webvan's terrible performance and impending bankruptcy. He left the company with the promise of $375,000 annually for the rest of his life, in addition to a $6.7 million loan from the company to pay taxes on a Webvan stock purchase, which was forgiven.

I won't comment on Shaheen's leadership of Webvan except to note his timing in taking the job was horrible, given the quickness with which the bubble burst after his decision. But it had all the earmarks of an executive making the wrong move for the wrong reasons.

Sadly I've seen companies with healthy contracts turn into ones with unhealthy agreements. An example is Whittman-Hart, which at one time was one of the finest information-technology consulting firms around. They hired great people and offered attractive career paths. The culture was fun, collaborative, and progressive. They had well-designed mechanisms to manage performance and provide feedback. Their compensation program was thoughtful, articulate, and predicated on paying people for performance.

Like all too many technology companies, Whittman-Hart got infected with the belief that the stock market held the key to explosive growth and vast wealth. The company granted stock options, went public, and people started to think they could make a lot of money in a short period of time. The employment contract took a turn for the worse, but the core health of the company was still intact. Then at the height of the dot-com boom, the company changed its name to MarchFirst and acquired US Web, a conglomerate of Internet firms, for a huge price. They made the acquisition in hopes of riding the Internet wave. Their new businesses, however, were more promise than substance. Within 18 months, it sought bankruptcy protection.

In time the more desirable remnants of the company were bought by Divine Interventures, a software and technology consulting firm whose culture was nothing like that of the old Whittman-Hart. From a long-term strategy, the focus shifted to quarter-by-quarter results. Everyone seemed to be in a perpetual state of panic or near panic with one fire drill after another. This is typical of companies that have lost coherent vision beyond the quest to get the stock price up. Employees and management alike focus on quarterly earnings (or lack thereof) and the stock market's response.

Whittman-Hart was not alone in its fate. This was and is true of many, many companies. In fact today the business landscape is pockmarked with these imploded companies, some of which are still surviving. The long-term survivors will be those that create a broader, healthier, long-term contract with their employees.

LESSONS OF THE NEW ECONOMY

Today companies have an opportunity to learn from past mistakes and successes. Companies with poor employment contracts have a chance to begin anew with healthier and more balanced agreements. This does not mean we should—or can—turn the clock back to the 1980s and declare it business as usual. On the positive side part of the exuberance we felt in the 1990s was completely rational. The hope we had for the new economy was not all mass hysteria; there was and is some truth and substance to it. There were, indeed, lessons to be learned from the new economy:

1. The value of human capital. We preached, learned, and came to believe we had entered the age of human capital. We recognized the contribution of people who are at least as valuable, if not more so, than physical assets and financial capital. This was absolutely true and remains the case today.
2. The need to reflect the value of human capital through some type of investment vehicle. The widespread granting of stock options to employees was not just a fluke nor did it only serve to assuage some guilt about enormous executive grants (although it did that too). Broad-based option grants were and are a very profound statement about the value of human beings—individually and collectively.
3. The onset of the information age is real. Technology greatly enhances and improves the value and magnitude of human contribution. It also makes it faster and far easier to spread and share information, ideas, and knowledge.

MAKING HEALTHIER CONTRACTS

Acknowledging the importance of human capital, enhanced by the use of technology, companies can design and implement healthy contracts with employees. To begin with, we must first acknowledge that the line between the company and the employees is increasingly blurred. The "us versus them" relationship between employers and employees (typified in the traditional union/management conflict) is in transition. Both companies and employees are beginning to recognize they are in this together. Employees are no longer cogs in a production wheel or interchangeable parts. Individually and collectively, people make a varied and valuable contribution to the organization. This is the basis of the healthy contract.

The first premise is if human capital is one of the most valuable assets, if not the most valuable asset of a company, then people need to be treated as such. In a state-of-the-art production facility, the company spends an enormous amount of time, resources, and money to make sure the plant is operating at peak efficiency. Every facet of its output is monitored. Based on that feedback, the production process is constantly being adjusted to improve the operation and squeeze out every increment of productivity. In the age of human capital, we have to pay the same level of attention to people, their well-being, their growth and development, and their output.

This starts with how people are hired. Companies recruit and hire people based upon skills, competencies, behaviors, and abilities. Then people are given opportunities that match their skills, proficiencies, and even their personalities, emotional predisposition, motivational level, and risk tolerance. They must be provided with good direction and management; frequent, objective, and useful feedback; and clear opportunities to challenge themselves in their areas of weakness so that they can grow and improve as assets of the organization.

To fully develop their human capital, companies must offer training opportunities to all employees and executives to grow and develop. To some extent this is already happening not only at the top echelon of Corporate America but also in small businesses.

Bob Wright of the Wright Institute for Lifelong Learning in Chicago has created a remarkable organization for fostering personal growth and development. Most importantly he practices what he preaches. For example while administrative staff make a relatively low salary by corporate standards, an additional 25 percent or more of their pay is variable based on their productivity and contribution to the organization. Moreover Bob provides his staff with a remarkable amount of training to further their personal and professional development. Someone making $40,000 a year may receive $20,000 to $30,000 worth of training. These individuals grow and develop more in one year than employees at other firms do in 5 or 10 years. Regardless of where their careers take them, their experience at the Wright Institute helps them focus more clearly on what they want out of life and gives them the courage and skills to pursue it. This is no accident. Employee development is an important part of Wright's business purpose and philosophy.

In my own career I recall when I worked as a compensation consultant with Sibson & Company, a premier compensation-consulting firm. Sibson had one of the most rigorous and meaningful performance evaluation processes I've ever seen or been a part of. At Sibson, we expected a lot from our employees, and twice a year we conducted thorough reviews that included both written and verbal feedback. Evaluations were based not only on each employee's financial contribution but also on how well he or she exemplified and promoted the values of the firm. For every criticism made or shortcoming cited, a developmental goal was suggested.

Companies today expect much different types of contribution from employees. On one hand employees are expected to work hard and produce results according to prescribed expectations. On the other they are expected to think independently and to take appropriate risks. At the same time employees must be able to operate within teams. Thus the three criteria for employees are to be: good leaders, good followers, and good team players. Admittedly this is an extremely complex skill set. However, effective compensation systems—in tandem with good performance management and performance measurement systems—should encourage and reward all of these desired behaviors and results.

THE ROLE OF COMPENSATION

A company's compensation program, along with its benefits package, retirement plan, and performance-management system, are the tools used to define and execute its contract with employees. Each component delivers something of value in exchange for some service, action, or result. Companies should be as explicit as possible about what each component delivers and what is expected in return—in other words what are we paying and what are we paying for?

As Figure 9-2 illustrates the basic components of an employee-employer contract are defined by compensation and benefit programs. Clearly there are other elements of the contract, and it is beyond the scope of this book to define all aspects of the employee-employer relationship. The point is that the contract is multifaceted and complex, and stock options or other equity incentives are only one component.

The Lesson of the Stock Option

What we've seen and experienced in the technology and dot-com revolution is the spread of company ownership, albeit through the questionable means of the stock option. The cynical person may dismiss that as only an employee appeasement since executives received the bulk of the options (with some estimates as high as 60 to 80 percent of all the options granted in some broad-based, company-wide plans). Employees were only given a token amount of options, the cynic says, to feel as if they had a piece of the action and to justify the executives getting even more options.

The idealist, however, says something has fundamentally changed. Companies have, indeed, recognized the value of the individual employee—beyond just a paycheck and the occasional incentive. By offering an ownership stake, companies have made employees a part of the organization.

These are two distinct sides of the argument. The question now is should standards for executive compensation apply to mid- and lower-level employees as well? The answer is: it depends on the philosophy of the organization. In other words if the purpose of the organization is only to make money or maximize shareholder wealth, then employees are just a means to that end. However if part of the purpose of the organization is to foster the growth, development, welfare, and wealth of the human element of the business transaction, then terms and conditions need to be established for those employees. That may include, over time,

FIGURE 9-2

Types of Compensation

Type of Compensation	Specific Form	What Is Provided?	What Is Expected?
Salary	Fixed amount in equal bimonthly payments; in cash. Subject to annual review and possible increase.	Challenging work. Clear expectations. Promotional opportunities. Secure, regular, predictable income. Additional increases based on "merit" and COLA.	Performance of basic responsibilities. Growth in skills and competencies. Basic adherence to company culture and norms.
Annual Incentive	Annual, variable payment in cash based on individual, team, and company performance.	Variable, lump-sum payments to supplement income, possibly significantly.	Achievement of specific goals, objectives, and results. Contributing above and beyond basic duties to overall company success.
Benefits	Health-care insurance, vacation, holidays, sick days, etc.	Security for provision of needed health care. Lifestyle maintenance. Peace of mind.	Loyalty and commitment. Content, secure workers. Healthy employees.
Retirement Plan	Pension Plan or 401(k) plan or profit-sharing plan.	Ability to retire. Ease of savings accumulation. Funding for major expense or retirement.	Loyalty and commitment. Long-term retention.
Long-Term Incentive	Stock options, restricted stock, or other cash-based incentive.	Long-term capital accumulation. Retirement enhancement funding. Funding major expenses. Building investment portfolio.	Long-term commitment. Long-term focus on performance. Holding company's best interests. Adding value to the company.
Performance Appraisal/ Management	Annual or semiannual performance reviews, feedback, coaching, and training.	Valuable and useful feedback, coaching, development, and training. Promotion opportunities.	Continued growth and development, according to career path, of skills and behaviors valued by the company.

employees becoming owners, which ties their long-term wealth and well-being to the organization itself.

This concept is nothing new. Sears, Roebuck did it more than 50 years ago with a highly successful profit-sharing plan invested in company stock. It was an effective way to tie together the interests of employees and the employer, and everybody involved understood the concept. It was not vastly different from broad-based stock options.

Another notable example is a Spanish company, Mondragón Corporación Cooperativa, which is one of the largest companies in Europe. A cooperative, its employees own Mondragón. This $6 billion-revenue company has a very different mission and purpose than the typical company, owing to its ownership and heritage. Mondragón was founded in the 1930s in the Basque region of Spain, which at the time was extremely poor. A cooperative was formed in partnership with a local businessman with the mission to develop, train, employ, and elevate the whole community. Ultimately the profits made from this very profitable company are used for the care of the employees, including their retirement, and the betterment of the community.

That's not to say the typical American corporation should be run the same way as a European cooperative. However there are important lessons to be learned from the Mondragón model. All companies must decide how much of their purpose is to serve the well-being, growth, and development of the people who work for them. Are employees considered disposable cogs in the company machine? Or are they truly integral to the function of the organization? While this is not a simple question, each company must answer it. If companies do put a value on human capital, then they must address whether and how employees should share in ownership, management, and governance.

Stock options go at it backwards, doling out a ticket to ownership in hopes that it will make employees and executives think and act like owners. A far healthier approach is, first, to encourage the kind of action and behaviors that warrant having the chance to become owners. Motivating employees to think and act like owners, however, is one of the biggest challenges of corporate managers today.

Helping Managers Manage

Managing other people is difficult, awkward, confusing, and emotionally challenging. Most of us don't do it well; we have far more management mistakes than triumphs. Management is also harder these days than in the past, when in a traditional "command and control bureaucracy" the jobs and roles were more clearly defined.

In a modern organization, it's not the job that is reviewed but the person performing it. It is far more difficult to measure human qualities than to determine whether a specific job was completed. Furthermore the process of delivering feedback is personal and touches upon people's emotions, feelings, and desires. Few companies do this very well.

Some of the worst managing is done at the board level, particularly when it comes to reviews of CEO performance. Based on my experience I would say at least half of all public companies don't do CEO reviews while approximately 30 percent do only a cursory job. This leaves about 20 percent of public companies doing a decent job of CEO reviews.

Because managing others is so difficult and often is not well done, there is a tendency in Corporate America to think that compensation and incentives can take care of that for us. Many managers would love to have a compensation system measuring and rewarding every dimension of employee performance. The fact of the matter is a compensation system cannot replace good management. But it can enhance good management.

Compensation is an extremely powerful management tool that should be used to reinforce appropriate and desired behaviors to produce targeted results. That's essentially what it's for: providing a reward or a consequence for particular actions. The job of every manager is to set boundaries on one side and targets and a vision on the other. In this context compensation is a powerful mechanism for setting challenging goals and rewarding the achievement of those goals.

Stock options do have their place in a system of rewards and incentives. For example they are extremely useful in a cash-strapped start-up, as long as their use is clearly communicated. They also have a place as part of a balanced incentive package, or as a way to share ownership with employees over time. However in most corporations, options—especially large quantities of fixed-price options—are an extremely blunt, ineffective, and inefficient instrument. They offer only rewards, with no commensurate consequences.

THE ROLE OF LONG-TERM INCENTIVES

Just as it's important to set solid goals and consequences in a reward system on an individual basis, it must also be done at divisional and corporate levels. This is often the role of the long-term incentive. The purpose of long-term incentives is to reinforce organizational goals that groups of people, company divisions, or the entire corporation must work toward. Spurred on by a long-term incentive package, executives and employees pursue a small set of high-level goals over a multiyear time horizon. These incentives also serve to align the personal financial success of the individuals with that of the company. If the organization does well, the employees do well. If it doesn't, they don't either. It's a healthy, straightforward arrangement.

Long-term incentives also have the potential to unify an organization in which there may be conflicting goals and competing interests. In many companies, for example, the executive in charge of manufacturing is almost always in some type of conflict with the executives in charge of marketing or finance. To bridge these naturally competing interests within the organization, there must be an overriding goal that ties all parties together. Companies have tried to do this with stock options, and sometimes they work well.

A far better way, though, is with incentives that reward performance and actions to achieve long-term goals. Most of us tend to have a short-term focus. It is a rare individual who focuses two to three years out. In an organization it's the CEO's job to plot a course over the next several years. Long-term incentives allow people within the organization to understand and implement a company's vision for the future. Moreover incentives also convert that vision into measurable results, with a significant monetary reward attached to them.

The beauty of long-term incentives is they do not have to be complex. Often they involve a very simple mechanism. But an elegant solution always looks simple when it's done well.

THE PRIVATE COMPANY

Compensation issues also confront privately held companies. However when it comes to executive compensation, particularly stock incentives, they operate very differently from their publicly traded counterparts. The experiences of private companies, which usually are run and managed by principal-owners with a longer-term and more personal view, offer some valuable lessons for public firms.

The most obvious difference between a private company and a publicly traded one is its ownership structure. It doesn't have publicly traded stock. Thus the allure of ownership looks and feels very different. At a private company there is no perceived magic of the market in which a stock can double or triple in value in a short time. Executives who work for a private company can't check the stock price daily in the newspaper or online to see how the company is doing and perhaps calculate their own paper fortune. There is far less transparency in the value of a private company but also no wild swings in value.

Private companies are usually managed differently than publicly traded firms. They are not managed for quarterly results but for the longer term. There is a different pace of business. (This also distinguishes long-time privately held companies from firms focused on going public.) Most significantly privately held companies tend to be run by the owners. The principals and the agents are usually the same people, meaning they don't have the same conflict as publicly traded companies.

Despite these differences private companies have not been insulated from the stock option issue. Over the past 10 years they have felt pressure in the war for talent. To compete with publicly traded companies that have used stock options to attract and retain executive talent, many private companies have felt the need to offer stock options or something like it.

But an ownership stake in a publicly traded company is far different than a stake in a private concern. With few stakeholders in a private company, ownership is often jealously guarded. As a result private companies are usually far less generous when it comes to offering ownership than public companies. They also tend to give long-term incentives to fewer people. Furthermore private companies typically focus on financial performance as the criteria for rewarding talent. Even if they do focus on the equity value of the company, it is usually based on a formula derived from financial performance.

Clearly private companies have been far less concerned about the accounting implications of their compensation practices and more concerned about the true economics of the transaction. Long-term incentives are not paid out unless they have been clearly earned with increased performance. I have never worked with a private company willing to give out money or an ownership stake without demonstrable and measurable improvement in performance.

The experience of private companies serves as a powerful lesson for public companies. The requirement that long-term incentives, particularly those leading to ownership, must be earned through measurable results is a practice more public companies should adopt. In fact in a post-expensing world, I expect there to be convergence among the practices of private and publicly traded companies. Public companies, in some ways, will be moving toward the private-company model. That said the age of equity and ownership participation is not over. It's merely changing form. Instead of just giving away ownership through large stock-option grants, public companies will require that ownership be earned.

That doesn't mean private companies do not have to make changes. Private companies will continue to feel the competitive pressure to attract and retain talent and not to lose it to publicly traded companies. The allure of the public market over the last decade has drawn many people from private companies, at least partly because a lot of private companies have been loath to give up ownership. Equity stakes are often awarded slowly, grudgingly, and after executives have jumped through multiple hoops to earn them.

To be competitive in the ongoing war for talent, private companies will have to continue moving in the direction of developing creative ownership. In time this may be another point of convergence with publicly traded companies as they seek to develop and implement new stock ownership concepts. There are many possibilities for private companies to consider. Ownership can be conveyed through options or restricted "phantom" stock, or special classes of stock that convey some aspects of ownership but not others to executives.

Ownership, however, is not to be given away indiscriminately. As private companies know and more public companies are learning, ownership is best earned over time. This not only recognizes the value of human capital, it also honors the value of the ownership stake. This balance is necessary for healthy contracts between a company and the employees who make up its most valuable asset.

WHAT DO YOU THINK?

- How important is the human element in your company's productive and value-creation processes?

  For example, if you work for a software-development or professional services firm, people are far and away the most valued element. On the other hand in a steel mill or a mining operation, physical capital and raw materials significantly outweigh the importance of people.

- How is the relative importance of people demonstrated in your company?

  How is this reflected in your training programs, performance evaluations system, work/life programs for employees, career opportunities? What is motivated and rewarded by compensation?

- What role does compensation play in the management of executives and employees?

  Is compensation used effectively to set goals, communicate priorities, delegate authority and responsibility, to give useful feedback, and hold people accountable? In what ways is your system ineffective?

VALUING PEOPLE AND THE PURPOSE OF THE CORPORATION

Stonyfield Farm, the leading manufacturer of all-natural and organic yogurt in the United States, sees philanthropic and environmental causes as good business. Stonyfield, which donates 10 percent of its profits every year to environmental charities and causes, follows a marketing strategy that combines its social, environmental, and financial missions. Additionally the company rewards executives and employees based not only on financial targets but also achievement of specific environment and social goals. Although still privately held, New Hampshire-based Stonyfield Farm agreed to sell an initial 40 percent stake to Group DANONE, a French consumer products company. I talked with Gary Hirshberg, co-founder, chairman, president, and CEO of Stonyfield Farm, about compensation, employee ownership, and social responsibility.

Delves: Part of my mission in writing this book is to foster positive change from within. As part of that I've had to ask the question, what is the purpose of a corporation? There is a mainstream belief that the purpose is to maximize shareholder value.

Hirshberg: I think that to be in business for the sole purpose of delivering shareholder return is irrelevant if not immoral. I look at every problem on the planet and see that it exists because business has not made the solution a priority. Therefore, to me, it's the role and responsibility of business to address how we advance shareholders' and stakeholders' total returns—which includes assuring that their grandchildren are going to have a habitable planet. To think narrowly in terms of just taking a profit out is to be so myopic and short-term, and is, in fact, a disservice. When I set out 20 years ago in this business and with that notion, I admit it was a hypothesis. It was a question, not a statement: Could I run a business run by that principle, and be successful at the same time? Twenty years later—in fact 15 years later because it happened five years ago—I could say and can still stay that this idea of using business to address and take responsibility for addressing common concerns of a societal or community nature is a profoundly successful business strategy.

Compensation fits into that. Part of what we do here is pride ourselves in participation, and that means participation in the gain also, which is not to say that we give up anything in terms of what our shareholders get or even what our top management gets. We're a very hierarchical, very traditional company. Top executives are paid more than folks at the bottom of the ladder. But we think it's important to attempt to close the gap between the top and the bottom, and we think it's also important that the people who are contributing to the gain also share in it.

Delves: How have you balanced these views and goals with your efforts to provide an acceptable return for your shareholders? Do you deal with your investors differently than, say, a publicly traded company?

Hirshberg: Because we market differently to the consumer, we also have attracted a different kind of investor. They tend to be long-term players with more patient capital-investors who are committed to wanting to make a difference. When we told them that 10 percent of our profits were going to environmental causes and when we told them that 20 percent of our ownership was going to go to people who were building the company, they had to swallow these things, which we would know in conventional parlance as "discounts on that capital return." But the contention that we made—and these particular shareholders were sympathetic to this contention—is that this would guarantee a stronger and more likely return for them. We don't have a control for this experiment, but I can tell you that none of the shareholders has complained about the truly remarkable returns that we've gotten for them.

The other answer to your question is the Danone deal resulted in top brand value and top return on investment for the investors and also a gain for employees because we have continued independence because we have a pledge of non-interference. Finally, it's a win for the consumer, because the notion of protecting the community from toxins in the soil, water, and food that have been at the heart of our mission have been thoroughly and completely endorsed and embraced.

Delves: You obviously view your employees—your human capital—as a vitally important part of the business. What kind of incentives do you offer them, and how do you reward them for their performance?

Hirshberg: We observe a three-legged stool model. First we have open-book management. We put the P&L up on a big board and explain it to everybody. The profit sharing or MBO (management by objectives, or goals used for performance evaluation) or some kind of paying for performance is the second leg. And the third leg is ownership participation.

The profit-sharing plan gives a short-term focus and a reward for short-term results. We don't want to reward just the short term, however. That's where the stock ownership piece comes in. Plus, we have an aggressive match for the 401(k) plan (and an employee stock purchase plan). It's hard to get people to put aside capital for the long term. We spend a lot of time encouraging people to participate. About half of employees participate in the stock purchase plan.

Delves: You measure performance or success based upon dollar profits, customer satisfaction, community goals and the environment. How do you measure your success in all these areas? Do you pay people based upon them or just for the profit achieved?

Hirshberg: We pay for all because we have to. To measure our environmental progress, we've used outside environmental auditors. What that entails is the amount of waste going to the landfill. As for the electricity, water, and all the other resources, you measure them in your utility bills. We set goals and we have an environmental incentive that is part of everybody's participation in the profit-sharing plan. In terms of consumer satisfaction and revenues, especially, all senior managers get their bonus tied to a combination of revenue and EBIT (earnings before interest and taxes). In the case of the manufacturing plant, they don't get the profit-sharing plan, but a bunch of things that add up to the same. It would be safety, productivity, and consumer complaints.

Delves: What incentive or programs have you offered to executives and top management?

Hirshberg: We have a time-accelerated restricted stock award plan (TARSAP), which is offered to the top one-third of the company— middle, upper-middle, and senior managers, and of course myself— that has been probably the most aggressive program that we have and that's where the great incentive has been. The TARSAP has been a more aggressive opportunity where the acceleration feature is tied to bona fide business objectives. We did accelerate the TARSAP (based on performance) so that everybody would be fully vested earlier. That was a neat breakthrough. It created a lot of wealth for long-term employees; it's paid for college educations; it's paid for new homes and very serious life savings.

Delves: How have you used stock options?

Hirshberg: In the early going my partner and I had diluted ourselves down to a small percent of the company. (At the peak we had 297 investors). We had to do that to have the company survive. We were able to make the case to shareholders and they were big enough to accept it, that there would be very little motivation for us at that small percentage of ownership. So through the use of stock options, we and other senior managers were able to earn our way back up, not to our original positions but to a much stronger position.

Delves: That's excellent. You used the option plan for yourself and other senior managers to earn your way back into the company.

Hirshberg: We earned the options by performance. . . . Moreover we saw options as a tool not of compensation, which they ultimately are, but a tool of ownership and control. We believe that people need to have a figurative if not a literal sense of ownership to participate. In the case of many of my senior managers, I had to steal them away from a large company, and the options were seen as strictly compensatory. But on the other hand, they liked the fact that anything disclosed to shareholders would be disclosed to them. For many middle-level managers, it was the first and only stock ownership opportunity in their lives. It was a way to turn sweat into equity.

PART THREE

The Path to Accountability

CHAPTER TEN

Restoring Corporate Integrity

There are several reasons for the loss of confidence in American business. Three of the biggest are executive compensation, principles of corporate governance, and auditing and accounting issues. In this book we have focused mainly on the first issue: the state of executive compensation.

Executive compensation is a touchy and emotionally charged topic. Ever since I became a compensation consultant in the mid-1980s, I've paid close attention to how executive pay grabbed the headlines each proxy season, when companies release their proxy statements that include detailed compensation data for the top five executives. Every spring there are numerous stories in the business press about what top executives are paid—with all the expected commentary on the size of the salaries, bonuses, and stock option grants.

Unfortunately we have yet to seriously address the issue of escalating executive pay other than to say "oh my, isn't that a lot!" It's as if the shock and outrage over executive pay come with the territory. Somehow it's okay if people—including shareholders—shake their heads over how much money the top executives are paid. We have yet to determine and implement truly rational and widespread systems of paying CEOs and other senior executives what they are worth based on what they produce.

171

In the past 20 years there have been few developments of any consequence to mitigate the rise in executive compensation. The Securities and Exchange Commission (SEC) in the early 1990s significantly expanded and standardized the public disclosure of executive compensation. This was very well done, although it fell short of requiring companies to calculate the cost of stock options and include it in total compensation paid. Then in 1994 Section 162(m) of the Internal Revenue Code was passed. This new tax law imposed a $1 million limit on employers' annual deduction for the compensation of top executives (see Chapter 2). Since stock options were exempt from the cap, this turned out to be a fairly meaningless and largely dysfunctional piece of legislation. In fact it helped fuel the explosion of free stock option grants.

If for no other reason than to avoid further legislative meddling, business must change the way it structures, administers, reviews, and reports executive compensation. The Conference Board advocates changes in executive compensation. Its blue ribbon panel called The Commission on Public Trust and Private Enterprise has recommended "wide-ranging reforms to strengthen corporate compensation practices and help restore trust in America's corporations and capital markets."

In its September 2002 report on executive compensation, the commission stated, "There is a widespread perception of a lack of fairness since certain executives have garnered substantial compensation even as their companies and the retirement savings of their employees have collapsed."

When it comes to restoring corporate integrity, the expensing of stock options is an important move in the right direction. However it cannot happen in a void. Other steps must be taken to improve the integrity, fairness, and accountability of Corporate America. While the focus here will be on changes needed for healthier executive compensation systems, I will make note of developments in other areas as well.

There have been some encouraging movements along those lines, which deserve to be highlighted. For example in November 2002, General Electric announced a new corporate governance policy, which includes changing the composition of its board to increase independence. GE also discontinued the use of stock options as the equity portion of annual compensation for its board members. Instead GE's board decided that deferred stock units (DSUs) would be 60 percent of annual director compensation. DSUs will not pay out until one year after a director leaves the board. Most importantly when executives exercise their existing options, they are required to hold a significant percentage of those shares for a minimum number of years.

Another positive development, as noted in Chapter 8, is the decision by Coca-Cola in December 2002 to stop providing advance guidance on quarterly or annual earnings per share. Advance guidance refers to the practice of predicting the next earnings announcement, which exacerbates investors' overly short-term focus on quarterly results. As Chairman and CEO Douglas N. Daft said in a statement, "We believe that establishing short-term guidance prevents a more meaningful focus on the strategic initiatives that a company is taking to build its business and succeed over the long run."

These two examples highlight concrete steps being taken to improve corporate governance and financial integrity. All companies, I would argue, should take a critical look at their governance practices with the end goal of restoring and strengthening investor confidence. In the name of more accountable companies, there can be no better place to focus than on executive compensation. Consider these nine steps for a healthier organization.

RESTORING CORPORATE INTEGRITY: 9 STEPS TO A HEALTHIER ORGANIZATION

1. **Total Cost of Management.** Boards of directors need to change the metrics they use to assess executive compensation. In particular they must lessen their slavish reliance upon competitive practice and take a more holistic approach that looks at the total cost of management, which encompasses not only salary, bonuses, and incentives but also perquisites, benefits, retirement enhancements, and loans. Executive compensation should be based on the total cost of management relative to the performance of the company.

What, then, is the company's return on management? As discussed in Chapter 6, there are numerous ways to gauge this and to compare this measure with that of peer companies. This is absolutely possible. All that is required is commitment on the part of boards, management, and their consultants.

2. **A Realistic Downside.** Compensation must have a realistic downside—and potentially a dramatic one. In addition to rewarding performance, compensation practices must carry consequences when goals are not reached or when performance is poor. Unfortunately over the past 10 years we've seen significant upside and no real downside in executive compensation. Some studies by consultants have noted that cash compensation actually decreased slightly as the economy slowed. This is encouraging but the decrease was slight compared to the more substantial drop in company performance. If large portions of pay are at risk, as many companies claim, then the portion at risk should largely disappear when performance drops significantly. Executives must be in a position to lose money due to bad corporate performance if they are also going to be in a position to make substantial amounts of money for good performance. This downside should not just affect their pay but also their personal wealth.

3. **Better Disclosure.** We've come a long way but there are still some notable gaps, particularly when it comes to executive contracts, golden parachutes, and other severance agreements. The SEC significantly increased disclosure requirements for compensation of the top five executives in each corporation. However companies can still engage in an incredible amount of obfuscation to hide very substantial payments to executives in the event of their termination or even retirement. While salaries, bonuses, and long-term incentives are open to scrutiny by the public, boards and management can engage in "stealth compensation" by providing lucrative enhancements to

pension plans, health-care coverage, post-termination consulting agreements, golden parachutes, loans, special vesting on stock options, company-owned life insurance, gross-ups for taxes, etc. While some of these benefits must be disclosed, the rules and the format for disclosure are unclear enough that companies can effectively hide some very substantial benefits and payments. Unfortunately many of these payments do not come to light until there is a change in control or some type of transaction. In the case of an executive's retirement, they can usually escape disclosure entirely (except in the notable case of Jack Welch, whose extravagant benefits came to light in post-retirement divorce proceedings.) In fact a company can avoid disclosing substantial payments to one of its top five executives by making the payments after the person has retired and the information no longer has to be reported. To truly make total executive pay more transparent to investors, these disclosure loopholes should be closed.

4. **Relative Compensation Levels.** Boards and management must start to take seriously the relative levels of compensation paid within a company. They must ask themselves if the CEO should really be paid several hundred times the wage given to the average worker. According to industry studies CEOs of major corporations made an average of 419 times the pay of an average worker in 1999, up from 326 in 1997 and 42 in 1980. Until recently I've always felt that the so-called CEO pay multiple was an irrelevant, socialistic concept with no merit in a capitalistic society where market forces drive the price for all goods and services, including the price of management. However in the last 10 years of my career, the tenfold rise in the CEO pay multiple has offended even my capitalistic, free-market, University of Chicago sensibilities. Add to that the fact that several conservative, mainstream, and highly respected board members of major corporations have independently brought this issue to my attention. I think it's time we collectively start to

take it seriously. I do not know the answer, but I do believe that as a corporate society we are capable of addressing this issue in some intelligent ways.

5. **Board Members and Stock Options.** Reconsider granting stock options to the board of directors. This once seemed like an excellent idea. However if options are a questionable incentive for management because they induce inordinately short-term thinking and behavior, then they are doubly questionable for the board, which is supposed to have a longer-term and broader perspective than management. The real question to ask is what combination of retainer, incentives, and stock ownership provides the board with an appropriate longer-term but highly engaged perspective?

6. **CEO/Chairman Issue.** Consider whether the CEO and chairman should be the same or separate individuals. This is a highly debatable and controversial issue and depends on the purpose and roles of the board as illustrated in the Figure 10-1.

   Many private companies hire independent boards with independent or at least separate chairmen to advise them. One example is the Follett Corporation, the largest

F I G U R E   10-1

Role of the Board

Role	Separate CEO & Chairman or Combined Roles	Alternative to Separate Roles
Review CEO performance and determine CEO pay.	Separate	Independent compensation committee with independent advisors.
Empower, advise, and support CEO.	Combined	Boards staffed with diverse business experts. Strong empowered committees with authority, budget, and agenda.
Review the overall performance of the company and the integrity of its financial statements.	Separate	Independent audit and financial oversight committee with independent advisors and budget.

schoolbook distributor in the country, owned by four generations of one family. The chairman never holds the CEO position. While the CEO runs the company, the chairman manages relationships with the board and the various constituents of ownership, and focuses on the long-term purpose, direction, governance, and oversight of the company. This ends up being a fairly symbiotic relationship with each doing what he or she does best. The chairman does not engage in oversight directly but rather oversees the oversight—making sure the board has the proper composition, structure, tools, and advisors. The chairman also institutes regular performance reviews of the board itself. One of the most important aspects of the chairman's job is to manage the process of reviewing the performance of the CEO.

7. **Independent Advisors for Compensation Committee.** The compensation committee must have the budget and authority to hire its own independent advisors, including compensation consultants, lawyers, accountants, and economists. Good executive compensation is critical to running a company. Given all the decisions a board makes, executive compensation is among the most important and has tremendous impact. Executive compensation is the means by which companies attract and retain leadership. Further it sets the tone for the compensation philosophy, integrity, and accountability throughout the company. What happens at the top flows through the entire organization. Doesn't it make sense, therefore, that the compensation committee should have a large enough budget to do a very thorough, ongoing analysis of executive compensation? Since executive compensation is one of main tools with which the board runs the company, shouldn't it have state-of-the-art technology and metrics to measure how well the tool works?

   There is an inherent conflict of interest involving management and many compensation consultants. As the CEO and other executives hire and pay a compensation consulting firm to advise them on their own pay, management also pays the same firm to advise and inform the board on management's pay. This is hardly a recipe for independent advice and governance. This is further complicated by the lack of independence within the major compensation-consulting firms. In addition to providing compensation consulting, these firms also provide actuarial, benefit, and other human-resource consulting to the same companies. For example, a consulting firm may collect $50,000 to $100,000 in fees for a typical executive-compensation assignment from a corporate client. In addition, that firm would typically receive $1 million or more per year in actuarial consulting fees, and perhaps another $1 million in fees for benefits consultation and services from the same client. If auditing firms are suspect for their lack of independence due to consulting fees, then these compensation firms are equally suspect, if not more so.

8. **Stock Price and Compensation.** Sever the link between executive compensation and stock price performance. We've become far too enamored with stock price as the primary means of rewarding executives and the primary measure of company performance. As the boom and bust of the last few years has demonstrated, stock prices can swing wildly, with very little connection to the actions or the results produced by the company's executive team. True, meaningful measures are needed instead. The Conference Board commission suggests measures such as cost of capital, return on equity, economic value added, market share, quality goals, compliance goals, environmental goals, revenue and profit growth, cost containment, cash management, etc. These goals should be directly linked to the long-term strategy of the company.

9. **Other "Principals" of the Company**. Recognize that the principal-agent dynamic exists in corporations. However there are other "principals" than just shareholders. They are employees, customers, communities, and the environment, in whose interests management "agents" must also act. As I've said the purpose and mission of a

corporation is to provide a needed product or service, as well as to serve employees, the community, and the environment. Therefore these elements must be reflected in compensation as well. Then, by definition, it becomes the responsibility of the board, which provides the highest level of oversight, to be the steward of these interests, as defined by the company's mission and corporate values.

While I'm not an expert on board governance, I do know a lot about leadership and I'm an expert in executive compensation. I've been in many boardrooms for a wide variety of corporations, large, small, public, and private. I know good leadership and decision-making when I see it, and I've seen both good and bad. I believe over the last 10 to 15 years boards have improved the quality of their leadership and decision-making on executive compensation. More and better data are being provided and more pay is being placed at risk. Pay does go up and down based on performance—just not enough. Stock ownership and stock options were initially a move in the right direction, part of a widespread and contagious movement to align executive interests with the interest of shareholders. Unfortunately our tools were flawed, our methods imprecise and ineffective. As in any bold and ambitious undertaking, mistakes must be recognized and corrected if it is to succeed. The bigger and more important the undertaking, the bigger and more obvious the mistakes. In the case of U.S. executive compensation, and stock options in particular, we have made some massive mistakes with some massive consequences.

We cannot discount the magnitude and importance of the task we are engaged in. We are harnessing and directing what is probably the greatest power on Earth—the American economy. And the American economy is American corporations. If you think about it, any large corporation such as GE or Microsoft probably has greater global influence and power than the Roman Empire had at its zenith. I haven't done the math, but Bill Gates probably has more resources and greater ability to change the world than Julius Caesar did.

My point is not to glorify these companies and individuals but to emphasize the impact of managing managers well. The executive leadership of American corporations represents the most capable, skilled, ambitious, and well-equipped pool of talent ever assembled. The personal ambitions, self-interests, and desires of these individuals have massive potential. It is our job to harness, contain, direct, and enhance this massive power toward positive ends. It is our job to use the tools that govern all human beings—rewards and consequences—to guide our leaders in creating positive change that will benefit all.

WHAT DO YOU THINK?

- How does your company's executive compensation system instill and enforce accountability and integrity?

  In what ways can the accountability and integrity of your company's pay system be improved?

- Do your executive management and compensation systems incorporate meaningful consequences for undesirable behaviors and results?

  Is there a substantial monetary "downside" built into the compensation plan?

  How often does executives' total compensation decline significantly when goals and objectives are not met?

- Where does your company's compensation system provide unnecessary guarantees or safety nets that protect executives from the consequences of their actions?

THE ROLE OF THE CEO

John H. Biggs is the immediate past chairman and CEO of the Teachers Insurance and Annuity Association–College Retirement Equities Fund (TIAA-CREF). With more than $250 billion under management, TIAA-CREF has provided financial service to the faculty and staff of America's education and research communities for more than 80 years. As an institutional investor TIAA-CREF has taken a stand on various issues, including executive compensation and corporate governance. I discussed these issues with John Biggs in his office in New York.

Delves: What are some of the key issues in corporate governance and executive compensation?

Biggs: One of our hot buttons is there ought to be a performance standard for stock options.

Delves: I totally agree with you. Once we start having to expense stock options, then we can put in performance criteria because we won't be penalized for doing it. Some executives and boards may say, to heck with that. Let's go for something more straightforward. If that occurs, then we're going to end up with performance-vesting restricted stock, cash plans, and other incentives that are based on fundamental financial performance. Speaking of expensing stock options, you sit on the board of Boeing, which was one of only two companies that chose to expense stock options several years ago.

Biggs: When I came on the board, they had already made that decision. I was celebrating and saying, "Hurrah! It's a great thing to do."

Delves: Another question on the topic of corporate governance. What do you think about the role of the CEO today?

Biggs: I think the CEO job is complex and difficult. As one of my colleagues, "Dolph" Bridgewater, the former CEO of Brown Group, always says, "No great company was created by corporate governance. Great companies are created bygreat leaders." That's usually the chairman and CEO of the company.

Delves: Do you think that American companies should have a separate chairman and CEO?

Biggs: I have no problem with separating the jobs if that is what a company wants to do, if there is an independent director who wants to do that. But I don't think I'm prepared to lay it on a company as a better model—to put in a separate person as chairman, who is going to spend a major amount of time to construct the board agenda, to manage the information flow to other directors. . . . The independent chairman is part of the British system of not having a really strong CEO who will abuse his power. Do we think that the British system produces a better company?

Delves: As long as you've got a board that is aggressive and functioning well, there may not be an inherent need to separate the CEO and chairman positions.

Biggs: Right now we are laying on the American CEO model all kinds of limitations. For example we're encouraging the audit committee to be clear that it appoints the auditor and manage that relationship, not the CEO. We're urging the audit committee to take on all kinds of roles that it didn't have before, such as before earnings are released the audit committee has to approve them. For the compensation committee, there are also lots of recommendations. They have to be independent. They have to be skeptical and so forth. The nominating committee has to make sure the CEO does not go out and name his buddies to the board. All those things are being done. One of the things the New York Stock Exchange is requiring is that independent directors meet privately on a structured, regular basis—without the CEO.

I don't believe any of these changes weaken the power of the CEO but rather strengthen the role of the board in its oversight. I don't believe many responsible CEOs would challenge the importance of the board overseeing the financial reporting process and the major personnel issues of corporate leadership. I think they would feel definitely weakened if the board, through some sort of lead director, took over responsibility for the agenda setting, information flow, and general leadership of the board itself.

Delves: When it comes to corporate governance issues today, one of the most pressing questions is, why is executive pay so high?

Biggs: The reason is infectious greed. Compensation consultants are the guilty parties for helping to spread the infection. The big problem has been the way consultants have presented the market data on compensation.

Delves: I know. I have done my share of presenting data showing companies how they can pay at the 75th percentile. I think we've all been guilty of promulgating the leapfrogging effect.

Biggs: Another factor has been transparency. I believe it has had an unintended effect.

Delves: Interesting. The increased transparency—which in itself is a very healthy thing—has contributed to the "competitive scorecard effect."

Biggs: I have seen presentations by consultants at a number of compensation committee meetings including that of my own company. I have never seen a set of numbers that did not show that the CEO was paid well below the 75th percentile. In the case of financial services companies, such a number in the 1990s was always at the $10 million level or much higher if a consultant picked a narrower group. These were the estimates for moderate-size companies and not the giant complexes. It seemed to me that the effect was to encourage midsize financial institutions to pay their people at much higher levels.

Delves: When it comes to designing and implementing healthy compensation plans, I believe that compensation committees need to have their own budgets. They must be able to hire their own advisors to do the heavy-duty analysis that is required. The level of the analysis that gets done is often lightweight and superficial. The critical issue that must be addressed is, how much are we paying people and what are we paying for? We need to do this over a multiyear time horizon. Companies need to look at all the stock options that have been granted over three to five years. What happens when the stock goes up $1, $5, or $10? How much does an executive's wealth change? How does that influence his or her behavior? Has the risk/reward profile of that person been altered in a way that is beneficial to the company?

Biggs: Or has it simply created an obscene benefit?

Delves: Companies shouldn't be surprised that someone cashed in $50 million in stock options. They should know how many options their executives are sitting on, and how this relates to their performance.

CHAPTER ELEVEN

Vision for the Future

Writing this book has been an incredible adventure. Not only has it allowed me to fill in a few gaps in my own knowledge and understanding about executive compensation, but I've also had to resolve some contradictions in my beliefs. Executive compensation is a tremendously complex issue; there are no clear-cut, easy, or one-size-fits-all answers. Still that has not stopped me nor should it stop anyone else from trying to find the truth.

To the best of my ability and all vested interests aside, I have tried to discover and articulate the truth as I saw it. To do that I had to address the fundamental issues of stock options. What is the value of an option? How should the value of an option be recorded? What kind of incentive do options provide? I examined some underlying assumptions about why corporations exist and whether stock performance is really the ultimate measure of an organization's success. I also had to do some soul-searching of my own. In my 20 years as a compensation consultant, where have I contributed to the creation of inappropriate incentives? When have I been a party in the misallocation of corporate resources?

These are not easy questions to ask of ourselves. Nonetheless this kind of self-examination is exactly what we have to go through—not only to expose the mistakes of the past but also to envision a healthier future. As part of my own quest for knowledge and insight, I was fortunate to speak with many CEOs, board members, public officials, academics, and other thought leaders, each of whom has gone through a similar process of introspection and reflection.

There are many people of high caliber who are truly thinking about executive compensation. Looking beyond the surface issues, they have gone deeper, questioning the foundations, structure, and purpose of executive compensation. For them it is not enough to ask, "What are other companies doing?" It's about asking the tougher questions. What is the right, fair, and effective way to pay executives? What standards, criteria, and values are communicated through executive compensation? What behaviors and attitudes should be encouraged? What are the appropriate rewards?

THE POWER OF THE CORPORATE EXECUTIVE

Truth be told corporate executives are among the most powerful people in our country, perhaps even in the world. Because we are a democracy, and corporations are basically democratic, we have bestowed power upon these executives. This "right of kings" is very crucial to defining the values of our society. It is no minor point.

This came to mind while reading *The Guns of August* by Barbara Tuchman, who notes that in 1910 most countries—with the exception of the United States and France—were still ruled by monarchs. Many rulers of these royal dynasties were related to each other and endowed by vast wealth through birthright and general consent of the population. All of that came to a crashing end by 1920 when most monarchies were replaced by democracies or Marxist/Communist rule.

To some degree in our modern world, monarchies have been replaced by corporate rulers, whom we collectively endow with an inordinate amount of responsibility and a commensurate, inordinate amount of wealth. I'm sure Jack Welch is worth more than a good number of pre-1900 European potentates. The downfall of kings, however, serves as an important lesson and warning for today's corporate royalty. A century ago, a more enlightened populace began questioning what the crowned heads actually contributed, as opposed to what they cost.

Today there is a strangely similar sentiment in Corporate America. Shareholders and activists are seeking to have more say and hold more sway in corporate policies, including compensation matters. The sense of outrage over the state of executive pay is real. Why do corporate leaders make so much? Should the CEO really be paid more than 400 times the average worker? (That did not happen, of course, because the average worker's pay went down.) The public is aghast at these pay levels, and yet few people in the executive ranks seem to want to do anything about it. But this apathy only perpetuates the problem and must stop now. For the well-being of Corporate America, it's essential that we all work together toward a healthy executive compensation system.

A VISION FOR THE FUTURE

In my lifetime I want to see executive compensation become rational and truly based upon performance. When we read about CEOs cashing in stock options for tens and hundreds of millions of dollars in addition to multimillion-dollar cash compensation packages or cashing in golden parachutes for $10 million, $20 million, or more after a poor-performing company is sold, we know that these packages are just not fair. Our instincts tell us this is neither right nor reflective of what these people are worth. When the average CEO's pay jumps from 40 times the average worker's to more than 400 times in 20 years, we don't have to be economists to know this is not just some mathematical aberration.

Below the executive level the market for talent is much more rational and generally follows the rules of supply and demand. For example when there is a shortage of nurses or electrical engineers, the market pay rate for these jobs rises. Demand then prompts more students to graduate with nursing and electrical engineering degrees. When the supply of professionals increases, the market pay rates even out again. This occurs as long as there is no disruption or limitation of market forces.

Given that pay rates for executives seem to only go up, it's obvious something is seriously wrong with the market for executive talent and, more broadly, for company management. While the United States prides itself on being the leading free-market, capitalistic economy in the world, we do not really have a free market for management in this country. Nor is executive pay based on a true market clearing price (the price at which all goods and services will be sold) for company management. Instead, like OPEC, there are controls on the system to keep the price of management artificially high. While the exact problem is uncertain, I have some strong suspicions that include the following:

1. Boards determine CEO pay, which is used as the benchmark for all other executive pay. Executives' pay increases with the rising tide of the CEO's pay. As I have noted earlier, most boards are populated by CEOs and executives of other public companies and are selected for their board positions by the CEO. They are not the most likely bunch to seriously challenge the CEO's pay or question the CEO's tenure.

2. Consultants who are hired by management typically advise board compensation committees. Remember if the CEO's pay goes up, so does the pay of the managers who hired and paid the consultant. This is hardly a free-market arrangement.

3. Compensation consultants provide management and the board with competitive data that has a number of limitations:

   a. It is usually annualized, looking at only one year of compensation instead of multiple years.

   b. The data are often focused on one, two, or three components of compensation but rarely reflect the total picture, including benefits, retirement, and, especially, contracts, and parachute agreements.

   c. The data focus on each person separately, instead of looking at the total cost of management.

   d. The data encourage leapfrogging, by which each company wants to pay in the top half or top quartile of all companies.

4. Regulations put in place in the 1960s and again in the 1980s severely restrict the ability of shareholders to quickly organize and replace management. This may be the most insidious of all of the limitations on the free market for executive talent. The belief that corporate

raiders and takeovers are bad, or at least suspect and dangerous, is deeply engrained in our culture.

5. Executives are remarkably well protected from losing their jobs. Today the typical senior executive of a public company stands to receive a golden parachute of *three times* salary and bonus, plus immediate vesting of all stock options, if the company is sold and they are terminated. Many CEOs stand to receive this payment even if they are not terminated after a takeover. I used to think this was normal, acceptable practice. Now that I run my own business and face the whipsaw of the open market on a daily basis, I think this is truly bizarre. If this level of protectionism is not a blatant restraint of trade, I don't know what is.

6. Stock options have also clearly played a role in the "un-free" market for management. All of the above factors work together to seriously weaken the ability of shareholders to influence and change the composition or compensation of the executive team. They exacerbate the principal-agent problem. Thus we have a situation in which management is relatively unfettered in giving shareholder resources to themselves in the form of stock options while never accounting for the magnitude of the gift. Not only is the fox watching the hen house, the farmer is unarmed and locked in his farmhouse. No free market at work here.

I wish I could point a finger of blame at some group, company, or person for this mess. But, as Pogo said, "We have met the enemy and he is us." Just as you can't drive by the smoke-belching steel mills in Gary, Indiana, in your shiny steel car (which wouldn't exist if it weren't for those steel mills) and say "look at *those* bad polluters," I don't believe that most of us can point a finger and say, "look at those bad payers." This is a problem we have created as a business community. However for the sake of the long-term health of our business community, it must be fixed.

The ideal result would be for people to read in the newspaper about how senior executives of public companies are being paid and, instead of rolling their eyes, they would have a warm feeling that all is right in the world. Their instincts would say, "That makes sense," or "That person deserved to make so much money," or "That board really did the right thing in cutting their executives' pay."

This is totally possible. Throughout the book, I have mentioned various prescriptions for change. But there are a few that are absolutely critical to a future with healthy and rational executive pay.

1. Board compensation committees should be independently advised. They should have their own budgets and should hire compensation consultants and other advisors who are independent from those used by management. Many will argue that this will set up a contentious and adversarial relationship between management and the board. This is not necessarily a bad thing. In order for the management-board relationship to benefit the company and shareholders, it *should* be adversarial. Free-market exchanges are by nature contentious, and as such result not only in market prices (and market pay levels) but also in more effective and creative solutions.

2. Board compensation committees should request and receive much more comprehensive data and analysis on the total cost of management over a multiyear time horizon, compared to various measures of performance and compared to other companies.

3. The link between pay and stock performance must be severed. While a component of compensation should be based on the long-term performance of the stock, most of the pay and incentives should be based on strategic, financial, and other critical measures of the company's performance.

4. Companies should have a highly effective performance management process for senior executives and the CEO. If not, then pay should be determined in a highly formulaic way, whereby increases and decreases in performance directly result in significant increases and decreases in pay.

5. Options should be expensed. There are many ways the expense can be determined and I'm somewhat indifferent as to how as long as (A) we have an expense, (B) it's a reasonable reflection of the value and cost to the company, and (C) we implement it very soon. Regardless of how the expense is determined, it is imperative that management and boards fully assess the true economic cost of options to the company and are vigilant in making sure the shareholders are getting a return on this rather substantial investment.

In all of this we can't lose sight of the fact that compensation is a management tool. Its primary purpose is to empower the board of directors, the CEO, and the management team to run healthy and robust companies. To do that effectively they must be given compensation tools that challenge people; that communicate goals, objectives, and direction; that integrate into a tight accountability system that provides feedback; and that deliver rewards and consequences in a way that helps people perform better and develop as individuals.

For me, as for a great many other people, the place where I have the most growth and challenge, excitement, disappointment, and reward is in my work. In this country so many people latch onto the myth that work is drudgery and that sitting in front of the television is enjoyment. That is absolutely false. People can and should experience great joy, satisfaction, and total engagement in their work. Our work should provide us not only with the means to support and enrich ourselves but also offer opportunities for continued learning and growth. Otherwise why are we here?

The work I have chosen has allowed me to take a position on executive compensation. It is both my privilege and my obligation to be part of the ongoing and in-depth discussion about the purpose and structure of executive compensation. My role as I see it is not just to point out the shortcomings of the past but, more importantly, to offer solutions and a vision for a healthier future.

Endnotes

1. The Conference Board Commission on Public Trust and Private Enterprise, Findings and Recommendations, Part 1: Executive Compensation (www.conferenceboard.com), September 17, 2002.

2. "Under the Radar: As CEOs' Reported Salaries and Bonuses Get Pinched, Many Chiefs Are Finding Ways to Increase Their Compensation," *The Wall Street Journal*, April 11, 2002.

3. Lowenstein, Roger. "Heads I Win, Tails I Win," *The New York Times Magazine*, June 9, 2002.

4. Market Report—Corporate Governance, California Public Employees' Retirement Systems (CalPERS), June 2002.

5. Useem, Jeremy. "In Corporate America, It's Clean-Up Time," *Fortune Magazine*, September 2, 2002.

6. Khurana, Rakesh. "The Curse of the Superstar CEO," *Harvard Business Review*, September 2002.

7. Collins, Jim and Porras, Jerry I. *Built to Last: Successful Habits of Visionary Companies*, HarperCollins, 1994.

8. Clark, Don. "Boss Talk: Contrary Intel Won't Expense Options, but It Will Offer Investors Data About Employee Grants and Executive Compensation," *The Wall Street Journal*, August 8, 2002.

9. Financial Accounting Standards Board news release, "FASB's Plans Regarding the Accounting for Employee Stock Options," July 31, 2002.

10. Strahler, Steven R. "An Icon Crumbles," *Crain's Chicago Business,* October 7, 2002.

11. Mann, Bill. "Are We Angry? You Bet," Motley Fool, www.fool.com, July 16, 2002.

12. Fox, Justin. "The Only Option (For Stock Options That Is)," *Fortune Magazine,* August 12, 2002.

13. Testimony before the U.S. Senate Committee on Banking, Housing and Urban Affairs, John H. Biggs, Chairman, President, and Chief Executive Officer, TIAA-CREF, February 27, 2002, (http://www.tiaa-crefinstitute.org/Speeches/spchfos7/02-27-02Biggs.htm).

14. Siegel, Jeremy J. *Stocks for the Long Run,* 2nd ed., McGraw-Hill, 1998.

15. Lashinsky, Adam. "The 'Real' Options Problem: The Earnings Hit from Expensing Is Only the Half of It," CNN/Money, (http://money.cnn.com/2002/07/17/commentary/bottomline/lashinsky/), July 17, 2002.

16. Smith, Adam. *The Wealth of Nations,* Everyman's Library Reissue Edition, 1991.

17. Jensen, Michael C. and Meckling, William H. "Self-Interest, Altruism, Incentives & Agency Theory," *Journal of Applied Corporate Finance,* Summer 1994.

18. Collins, Jim and Porras, Jerry I. *Built to Last: Successful Habits of Visionary Companies,* HarperCollins, 1994.

Index

special treatment for, 69–71, 79
stock options for, 38–40, 76, 78–79,
 117–118
State of Wisconsin Investment Board
 (SWIB), 12
"Stealth compensation," 174–175
Stock options:
 altering function of, 125–126
 for board of directors, 176
 cost components of, 68
 current problem with (*see* Problem with
  stock options)
 definition of, 5
 expensing of, xvii
 face value of, 8
 Four Guiding Principles for Evaluating,
  88–91
 future approaches to granting, 117–118
 as get-rich-quick schemes, 151–153
 granted by public companies, 70–71
 history of, 27–29
 indexed, 121–122
 "life expectancy" of, 89
 mega grants of, 8
 as misuse of corporate resources, 6–7
 perceived value of, 56, 83–85
 purposes of, 119–120
 reasons for proliferation of, 4
 as replacement for executive stock
  ownership, 34
 restricted, 20
 risk orientation with, 132
 for startups, 38–40, 70, 76, 78–79,
  117–118
 terms related to, 5
 underlying areas of concern about,
  65–66
 (*See also* Executive compensation;
  specific topics)
Stock ownership:
 benefit of, 142–143
 and quality of management, 111–112
 requirement for, by executives, 33–34
 risk orientation with, 132
Stock performance, 29
Stock price:
 appreciation of, xviii
 executive compensation link to, 178
 exercise, 5, 121–123
Stocks for the Long Run (Jeremy J. Siegel),
 86–87

Stonyfield Farm, 164–169
SWIB (State of Wisconsin Investment
 Board), 12

T

Takeovers, 29–33, 189–191
Taxes:
 income, 20
 and Internal Revenue Code, Section
  160(m), 34, 172
 valuation method for, 55
Teachers Insurance and Annuity
 Association–College Retirement Equities
 Fund (TIAA–CREF), 12, 180
Technology companies:
 as Arthur Andersen clients, 46–47
 culture of, 40–41
 during Internet bubble, 151–153
 reductions from options expensing by,
  49–51
 startup, 149–150
 stock option grants by, 3
 stock options for startups of, 38–40
 value of human capital in, 74
Term, option, 125–126
TIAA–CREF (*see* Teachers Insurance and
 Annuity Association–College Retirement
 Equities Fund)
Tort reform, 46, 47
Total cost of management, 173–174
Towers Perrin, 105–106
Traders, options valued by, 81–82
Trani, John, 24
Transparency, 183
"True-ups," 68, 72
Tuchman, Barbara, 186
Turner, Ronald, 76–80

U

Underwater options, 5, 122–125
 and overhang issue, 102–103
 repricing of, 123–125
Unexercised options, accounting for, 71–72
 (*See also* Overhang)
U.S. Steel, 19–20
US Web, 153

V

Valuation of options, 81–92
 with Black-Scholes pricing model, 56
 "Coca-Cola method" for, 86
 difficulty of, 57

About the Author

Donald P. Delves, CPA, is founder and president of The Delves Group, a consulting firm that helps companies improve employee effectiveness and performance by assessing and redesigning how they are organized, directed, and rewarded. With an MBA in finance from the University of Chicago, Delves has nearly 20 years of experience as an executive compensation consultant with several top firms including Sibson and Company and Towers Perrin. He has been featured in the Chicago Sun-Times, Strategic Finance, Director's Monthly, Crain's Chicago Business, and many other professional publications.